Reducing Rework in Officer Appointment Processes

KATHERINE L. KIDDER, ALBERT A. ROBBERT, JOHN JACKSON,
HANNAH ACHESON-FIELD

T0308615

Prepared for the Office of the Secretary of Defense
Approved for public release; distribution unlimited

RAND NATIONAL DEFENSE RESEARCH INSTITUTE

For more information on this publication, visit www.rand.org/t/RRA422-1

Library of Congress Cataloging-in-Publication Data is available for this publication.
ISBN: 978-1-9774-0608-8

Published by the RAND Corporation, Santa Monica, Calif.

Preface

Appointment scrolls are required for initial appointment of officers and for reappointment in a different grade, military service, or component. In some cases, they are necessary for appointment to a special branch or segment of a service's officer corps. The Office of the Secretary of Defense (OSD) processes over 2,500 appointment and promotion packages per year, and many require rework to correct administrative errors and incorrect information. Even without rework, the appointment and promotion scrolling process takes time, affecting the assignment timelines of officers needed in new capacities that require reappointment. The Office of the Under Secretary for Personnel and Readiness is interested in reducing the time needed to process appointments and the incidence of administrative errors, which result in time lost, administrative costs, and processing delays.

OSD asked RAND's National Defense Research Institute to evaluate the statutory and archival requirements for appointment scrolls, examine the military department and OSD processes used to meet these requirements, identify gaps and redundancies in the scrolling process that create excessive administrative burdens and delays, and recommend improvements to increase the efficiency of processes to produce nomination, appointment, and promotion scrolls for Secretary of Defense or Presidential and Senate action. In addition, researchers screened Title 10 of the U.S. Code and other related statutes to identify changes needed to appoint officers within a military service rather than within a component of a military service. The research reported here was completed in July 2020 and underwent security review with the sponsor and the Defense Office of Prepublication and Security Review before public release.

This research was sponsored by OSD and conducted within the Forces and Resources Policy Center of the RAND National Security Research Division (NSRD), which operates the RAND National Defense Research Institute (NDRI), a federally funded research and development center (FFRDC) sponsored by the Office of the Secretary of Defense, the Joint Staff, the Unified Combatant Commands, the Navy, the Marine Corps, the defense agencies, and the defense intelligence enterprise.

For more information on the RAND Forces and Resources Policy Center, see www.rand.org/nsrd/frp or contact the director (contact information is provided on the webpage).

Contents

Figures and Tables

Figures

Tables

Summary

Appointment scrolls—lists of individuals to be appointed—are required for initial appointment of officers and for reappointment in a different grade, military service, component, or, in some cases, a special branch or segment of a service's officer corps.[1] Appointment scrolls serve as the formal documentation of officer appointments as they are processed through the services, the Office of the Secretary of Defense (OSD), and (when applicable) the White House and the Senate. OSD processes over 2,500 appointment and promotion packages per year. Many of these packages require rework to correct administrative errors and incorrect information. Even without rework, the appointment and promotion scrolling process takes time, keeping officers from undertaking their new capacities.

The Office of the Undersecretary of Defense for Personnel and Readiness (OUSD [P&R]) is interested in reducing both the time needed to process appointments and the incidence of administrative errors. To evaluate the scope of the issue and possible solutions, we evaluated the statutory and archival requirements for appointment scrolls, examined the military department and OSD processes used to meet these requirements, and identified gaps and redundancies in the scrolling process that create excessive administrative burdens and delays. In this report, we recommend ways to increase the efficiency of processes to produce nomination, appointment, and promotion scrolls

---

1 An *appointment scroll* is a printed document listing the names of individuals to be appointed to an officer grade by the President, with the advice and consent of the Senate or the Secretary of Defense. In addition to the list of names, prefatory text indicates the grade to which the individuals are appointed and the statutory authority for the appointment.

for Secretary of Defense or Presidential and Senate action. In addition, we examined Title 10 of the U.S. Code, as well as other related statutes, to identify the changes needed to appoint officers to a military service instead of just to a component of a military service.

The appointment scrolling process creates frustrations for both the services and individual officers because of its complexity and the time it takes to complete. Without process improvements, these delays and possibly unnecessary administrative resource burdens are likely to persist.

Study Approach

We used a mixed-methods approach to characterize the errors and inefficiencies of the scrolling process. We first reviewed existing law, statutes, and U.S. Department of Defense (DoD) and service policies regarding the scrolling process to develop a baseline understanding of current requirements and processes. This required us to gain a systematic knowledge of how each service's appointments process functions in practice. We interviewed service representatives involved in the scrolling process, including military staff who oversee personnel processes and cadet commands. We also interviewed OSD staff, especially representatives from Officer and Enlisted Personnel Management (OEPM), to understand OSD-level processes and identify common challenges from the OSD perspective.

Using these interviews and available data, we identified the types of errors commonly associated with appointment scrolls, the point during the appointment process at which these errors were identified, and how these errors were redirected back into the processing system. We also estimated the amount of time and effort typically needed to rework the appointments.

Where available, we drew on data provided by OEPM regarding the frequency and types of errors for both original appointments and promotions. For original appointments, we analyzed aggregate data at the OSD level regarding the percentages of packages submitted with and without errors and compared processing times across the services for the years 2016 through 2019. For promotion scrolls, we analyzed data regarding error rates by service and component from 2016 through 2019. We interviewed service representatives involved in the scrolling process, including military staffs overseeing personnel processes and cadet commands. We also interviewed OSD staff, particularly representatives from OEPM.

Once the errors and procedural implications were identified for each service, we explored options for process revisions that could enhance efficiencies in the scrolling process.

Findings

Scrolling Requires Inputs from and Interactions Among Multiple Stakeholders

Each service's scrolling process is distinct,[2] but common elements exist across the services. Both the original appointment and the promotion scrolling processes for each of the services require interaction among several offices, including accession sources, personnel management offices or commands, and action officers interacting with OEPM. For original appointments, each service must coordinate inputs from all accession sources (including service academies, Reserve Officers' Training Corps, and Officer Candidate School). Each service must then draft a scroll and supply the requisite supporting documentation to OEPM, such as certifications of commissioning sources and completion or anticipated completion of "all requirements necessary to tender the original appointment" (DoD Instruction [DoDI] 1310.02, 2015, p. 6). The services must also identify all officers transitioning between active and reserve appointments and provide updated scrolls and supporting documentation, requiring inputs from reserve accession sources. For promotions, each service must provide a scroll and supporting documentation (such as promotion selection board results)

---

[2] The Army and Marine Corps scrolling processes are highly centralized; the Air Force scrolling process is moderately centralized; and the Navy scrolling process is largely decentralized.

to OEPM, requiring that service scrolling offices interact with offices or commands responsible for promotion processes.

Current Data Systems Limit Efficiency

Each service has developed its own data systems to manage its internal scrolling processes. Some services use commercial off-the-shelf systems; the Air Force has built on a system designed for a different purpose. The services provide draft scrolls and supporting documentation to OEPM. This process involves providing both paper and electronic files. OEPM uses its General and Flag Officer Decision Support System (DSS) to receive, track, and process these scrolling packages. The services' data systems are not interoperable with DSS, although the services have created workarounds to ensure that data are collected in templates that can be submitted to DSS.

DSS is limited in its functionality as a platform for OEPM to provide feedback and information back to the services. OEPM has created manual workarounds and templates (such as requests for information, Excel files with color-coded feedback, and detailed feedback documents regarding package issues) that can be uploaded to DSS for service review. However, DSS does not automatically notify the services of outstanding items requiring action; service staff must actively check for and pull uploaded documents.

Error Types and Implications

OEPM tracks error frequencies and types for both original appointments and promotions. Some errors are corrected within OEPM; others require correction by the originating service. Correction processes for all types of errors add to the processing timeline, but some errors require a more-time-intensive correction or clarification than others.

Administrative Errors

Administrative errors, such as misspelled names, missing or incorrect middle initials, and missing suffixes, require service correction on both the scroll and its supporting documents. The services must compare the name on the scroll with original documentation. Current practice across the services is to use the name as printed on the individual's Social Security card as the original source documentation. Services that maintain databases with scanned copies of source documents (such as the Air Force) are able to address these errors on a relatively short timeline and return the corrected package to OEPM for processing.

Header Paragraph Errors

DoDI 1310.02 stipulates the information that is required to be in the header of an original appointment scroll. The scroll must include the status of each person (officer, enlisted, or civilian) before their new appointment. DoDI 1310.02 also requires language indicating whether each appointment is *in* the grade (reappointment within the same grade) or *to* the grade (appointment to a new grade). These header paragraph distinctions are required by the Office of the General Counsel (OGC). The distinctions provide important information to scroll-processing offices, but they are not statutorily required on a scroll, and their inclusion creates opportunities for error and rework.

Incomplete Information Requiring Clarification

Other errors or questions require more-time-intensive corrections or clarifications. For example, officers transferring between components and awaiting a promotion in their original component might be simultaneously placed on an original appointment scroll and a promotion scroll. If the officer is processed on the appointment scroll before their promotion is tendered, the officer must be re-scrolled to the next-higher grade in the receiving component when their promotion is tendered. In other cases, original appointment scroll packages for individuals laterally commissioning (an original appointment at a grade higher than O-1) must include constructive service credit worksheets and documentation supporting the higher-grade appointment. Missing documentation delays package processing.

Reprinting Scrolls

Following DoD policy, each of the services provides electronic and printed copies of each scroll to OEPM when scroll packages are submitted.[3] However, it is possible that OEPM, OGC, or both offices identify errors in the scroll, returning both the electronic and printed copies to the service for correction. In the event that an error is identified, the services must correct the electronic file and reprint the hard copies of each scroll. Printing scroll copies at the latest point in the process (at OSD) has the potential to reduce rework.

Late Submissions

DoDI 1320.04 defines the OSD processing time as approximately 21 duty days (DoDI 1320.04, 2014, p. 13). OEPM data show that between September 2019 and February 2020, 21 percent of all original appointment packages (71 of 341) were submitted with less than two weeks between submission and service requirements for action. Late submissions strain OEPM staff by magnifying the effort required to complete the appointments by the desired date.

Recommendations

Using the findings listed above, we recommend the following three broad approaches to reducing rework:

1. **increased accountability:** providing more-complete feedback to the military departments on the types and frequency of errors
2. **increased automation:** using data processing to implement error-avoiding and error-trapping rules
3. **streamlining appointment processes:** eliminating rescrolling requirements when moving between regular and reserve components or between certain branches or corps within a service, and eliminating unnecessary distinctions in scroll headers, such as those that require separate scrolls for officers, enlisted members, and civilians.

---

3 At the time of writing, original appointments staff have stopped accepting hard copy packages and have been accepting them electronically because of coronavirus disease 2019–related maximum teleworking provisions within DoD. However, the packages still must be printed before submission to OGC.

These approaches could be implemented to some extent using the current DSS, but they would be much more readily accommodated by an improved DSS.

The following specific enhancements would be possible with the current DSS:

- using the DoD identification number in place of the Social Security number (SSN) as the unique person identifier; this would use DoD's preferred person identifier and allow the use of the Defense Enrollment Eligibility Reporting System (DEERS) as an authoritative source of names (including suffixes and middle initials) and prior military affiliations
- at the service level, adopting the online, single format scroll preparation system designed by OSD (or similar to the one used by the Air Force)
- using an Excel-based scroll worksheet (with field validation rules) to print scrolls at the latest possible point in the scroll production process
- streamlining the appointment process as described earlier
- capturing images of Social Security account cards as part of the source documentation for appointment packages (if SSNs continue to be used as person identifiers)
- maintaining sufficient error data to permit identification and diagnosis of prevailing problems.

Improving the DSS would make it much easier to comprehensively implement these enhancements. An improved DSS would provide a database searchable by individual (not only by scroll), would be interoperable with service-level systems, and would enable real-time feedback and tracking of the number and types of errors. In this improved DSS, coordination within the services and OSD could be done through searchable, easily circulated electronic files. Scroll printing could be deferred until all review, coordination, and corrective actions have been completed.

Acknowledgments

We extend our appreciation to current and former Officer and Enlisted Personnel Management (OEPM) staff, including Mike Melillo, CDR Matt Phillips (U.S. Navy), Col Todd Randolph (U.S. Air Force), Lindsay Reiner, Dale Bourque, and Cheryl Black for their engagement and thoughtful feedback over the course of the project.

We also thank Patricia Mulcahy, former director of OEPM, and William Atkinson, director of OEPM, for their guidance.

At the RAND Corporation, we acknowledge the invaluable feedback provided by John Winkler, Lisa Harrington, and Molly McIntosh. This report benefited from helpful reviews by Geoffrey McGovern and Brad Carson and editing by Jessica Wolpert.

Abbreviations

AFRISS	Air Force Recruiting Information Support System
CAD	call to active duty
CDB	career designation board
DEERS	Defense Enrollment Eligibility Reporting System
DMPM	Directorate of Manpower and Personnel Management
DoD	U.S. Department of Defense
DoDI	U.S. Department of Defense Instruction
DSS	General and Flag Officer Decision Support System
FY	fiscal year
GAO	Government Accountability Office
HQDA	Headquarters, Department of the Army
HRC	Human Resources Command
MCRC	Marine Corps Recruiting Command
MCRISS	Marine Corps Recruiting Information Support System
NDAA	National Defense Authorization Act

NPC	Naval Personnel Command
NRC	Naval Recruiting Command
OAB	Officer Accessions Branch
OCS	Officer Candidate School
OEPM	Officer and Enlisted Personnel Management
OGC	Office of the General Counsel
OSD	Office of the Secretary of Defense
OUSD (P&R)	Office of the Under Secretary of Defense for Personnel and Readiness
PLC	Platoon Leaders Course
PRIDE	Personalized Recruiting for Immediate and Delayed Enlistment Modernization
RA	Regular Army
RAPIDS	Real-Time Automated Personnel Identification System
RC	Reserve of the Army
RFA	request for appointment
RFI	request for information
ROTC	Reserve Officers' Training Corps
SASC	Senate Armed Services Committee
SMS	Soldier Management System
SSN	Social Security number
TAP	Transition Assistance Program
USUHS	Uniformed Services University of Health Sciences

CHAPTER ONE

Introduction

Appointment scrolls—lists of individuals to be appointed—are required for initial appointment of officers and for reappointment in a different grade, military service, component, or, in some cases, a special branch or segment of a service's officer corps.[1] Appointment scrolls serve as the formal documentation of officer appointments as they are processed through the services, the Office of the Secretary of Defense (OSD), and, when applicable, the White House and the Senate. OSD annually processes over 2,500 appointment and promotion packages, many of which require rework—making and responding to queries, making corrections, and returning packages for correction and resubmission—to address administrative errors and missing or erroneous information. Even without rework, the appointment and promotion scrolling process takes time, affecting the assignment timelines of officers needed in new capacities.

The Office of the Under Secretary of Defense for Personnel and Readiness aims to reduce the time needed to process appointments, as well as the incidence of administrative errors. To evaluate the scope of the issue and possible solutions, we evaluated the statutory and archival requirements for appointment scrolls, examined military department and OSD processes used to meet these requirements, identified the gaps and redundancies in the scrolling process that create excessive

[1] An *appointment scroll* is a printed document listing the names of individuals to be appointed to an officer grade by the President, with the advice and consent of the Senate or the Secretary of Defense. In addition to the list of names, prefatory text indicates the grade to which the individuals are appointed and the statutory authority for the appointment.

administrative burdens and delays, and recommend improvements to increase the efficiency of processes to produce nomination, appointment, and promotion scrolls for Secretary of Defense or Presidential and Senate action. In addition, we examined Title 10 of the U.S. Code and other related statutes to identify changes that would be needed to appoint officers within a military service rather than within a component of a military service.

The appointment scrolling process is required for nominations, appointments, reappointments, promotions, and retirements that require either Secretary of Defense approval or Presidential nomination with the advice and consent of the Senate. The process is necessary, but it creates frustrations for both the services and individual officers because of its complexity and the time it takes to complete. Without process improvements, these delays and possibly unnecessary administrative resource burdens, such as time delays, financial penalties, and other less tangible costs, are likely to persist. In particular, failure to complete reappointment scrolls in a timely manner could affect active component officers who want to transfer to a reserve component, resulting in breaks in service and the loss of potential reserve officers. Conversely, reserve officers who could transition to a regular component might be discouraged from doing so by the uncertain reappointment process.

Purposes of the Scrolling Process

The scrolling process serves two main purposes. First, the appointment scroll and its supporting documentation verify officers' identities. The appointment scroll must contain all the unique identifiers attached to an individual's identity. Current service practice is to use the officer's Social Security card as the baseline document for identity verification. The name on the appointment scroll (including middle names or initials and suffixes where applicable) and the last four digits of the Social Security number must therefore match the information listed on the officer's Social Security card. This practice enables the services and OSD to track an individual's progression in subsequent scrolls if necessary. The White House scroll template (Figure 1.1) depicts the format in which personally identifying information is provided.

Second, the supporting documentation justifies the officer's placement on a particular appointment scroll, ensuring that the officer's qualifications and past experience warrant a position in a certain grade. This information includes commissioning source documentation, constructive credit worksheets (for lateral commissions), and board reports (for promotion scrolls). Missing documentation raises questions regarding the validity of a scroll placement and can lead to delays in scroll processing.

Types of Scrolls

All officers appointed or promoted on both the active and reserve lists must be scrolled. 10 U.S.C. §531 outlines the original appointment authority for the President and the Secretary of Defense. The Secretary of Defense might sign original appointment scrolls for officers appointed to the grades of O-1 through O-3 on the active scroll and officers appointed to the grades of O-1 through O-5 on the reserve scroll

Figure 1.1
White House Scroll Template

I nominate the following named {PERSON} for appointment {IN/TO GRADE(S)} indicated in the {SERVICE} under title 10, U.S.C., {SECTION/SECTIONS}:

{GRADE/RANK}

LAST, FIRST M.	4567
LAST, FIRST M. II	8910
LAST, FIRST M., JR.	1112
LAST, FIRST M. III	1314
LAST, FIRST	1516

{GRADE/RANK}

LAST, FIRST M., JR.	1718

SOURCE: Document provided by the Office of Officer and Enlisted Personnel Management (OEPM).

(referred to as *Secretary of Defense appointments*). The President nominates, and the Senate confirms, all active scrolls for officers appointed to the grades of O-4 and above and all reserve officers appointed to the grades of O-6 and above (referred to as *Presidential appointments*; U.S. Department of Defense [DoDI] 1310.02, 2015, p. 7).

In addition to ensuring that scrolls are accurate and appointment packages are complete, the military department secretaries are responsible for providing memoranda recommending the officers for appointment. For Secretary of Defense scrolls, the memorandum must be addressed to the Secretary of Defense. For Presidential scrolls, the memorandum must be addressed to the Deputy Secretary of Defense for processing before the recommendation for nomination is sent to the White House (DoDI 1310.20, 2015, p. 14).

Methodology

We used a mixed-methods approach to characterize errors and inefficiencies in the scrolling process. We first reviewed existing law, statute, and U.S. Department of Defense (DoD) and service policies regarding the scrolling process to develop a baseline understanding of current requirements and processes. The most pertinent DoD policies are DoDI 1310.02, *Original Appointment of Officers* (2015) and DoDI 1320.04, *Military Officer Actions Requiring Presidential, Secretary of Defense, or Under Secretary of Defense for Personnel and Readiness Approval or Senate Confirmation* (2014). (Key provisions of these documents are provided in Appendix A.)

We needed to gain a systematic knowledge of how each service's appointment process functioned in practice. We interviewed service representatives involved in the scrolling process, including human resource and personnel offices, cadet commands, and military staffs overseeing personnel processes. We also interviewed OSD staff, particularly representatives from Officer and Enlisted Personnel Management (OEPM), to understand OSD-level processes and identify common challenges from the OSD perspective.

Once we identified the errors and procedural implications for each service, we explored options for process revisions that could enhance efficiencies in the scrolling process. After interviewing key stakeholders in appointment processes, we developed process maps depicting appointment actions at the service, military department, and OSD levels and used them to identify and evaluate potential process improvements. The process maps focused on specific processes within each service and component: accession, O-6 and below promotion, and general and flag officer promotions. (The process maps are provided in Appendix B.)

We also were able to identify specific pain points within the services, particularly the transition from active to reserve components and transitions within the health services communities.

Scope

The officer appointment and promotion processes involve the military services, OSD, the White House, and the Senate. Although the Presidential approval and Senate confirmation processes are important, we focus on the officer appointment and promotion processes internal to the services and do not examine the White House and Senate processes.

Using these interviews and available data, we identified the types of errors commonly associated with appointment scrolls, the point during the appointment processing at which these errors were identified, and how those errors were redirected back into the processing system. We also estimated the amount of time and effort typically needed to rework the appointments. We draw on data provided by OEPM (where available) regarding the frequency and types of errors for both original appointments and promotions. For original appointments, we analyzed aggregate data at the OSD level regarding the percentage of packages submitted with and without errors and compared processing times across the services for the years 2016 through 2019. For promotion scrolls, we analyzed data regarding error rates by service and component from 2016 through 2019.

After developing maps depicting current processes, we constructed idealized process maps in which friction points and rework are reduced throughout the scrolling lifecycle. In these maps, we address steps that are duplicated at different levels (for example, at the service, OEPM, and Office of the General Counsel [OGC] levels) and steps that, if moved to a later point in the scrolling process, mitigate inefficiency and rework.

Organization of the Report

Chapter Two outlines the processes and issues within OSD, particularly within OEPM. Chapter Three presents the existing processes and challenges within each of the services, identifying unique factors within each of the services and consistent challenges across the services. Chapter Four provides approaches to reducing rework. Chapter Five provides an analysis of potential updates to Title 10 that would eliminate the need to reappoint officers transferring between components. A requirement for this analysis is contained in the fiscal year (FY) 2020 National Defense Authorization Act (NDAA). Chapter Six provides observations and recommendations for process improvements.

We provide supporting material for this report through online appendixes. Appendix A provides a summary of DoD policies for original appointment and promotion scrolls. Appendix B provides the process maps. Appendixes C and D provide an Air Force scroll list worksheet and relationship edits used in an Air Force automated scroll preparation process. Appendix E provides line-in/line-out changes to Title 10, as recommended in Chapter Four, that would remove statutory distinctions between regular and reserve appointments.

CHAPTER TWO

Office of the Secretary of Defense Processes

OEPM processes all officer original and promotion appointments. Different staff members within OEPM focus on original appointments, promotions, and senior leader appointments. They receive appointment packages from various functions within the active and reserve components of the military departments, provide quality checks, correct or return for correction if necessary, and coordinate within OSD. The office prepares memoranda and scrolls for appropriate signatures by the Secretary of Defense or the Deputy Secretary of Defense.

OEPM staff observe the quality of original appointment and promotion packages received from each of the services and record the types of errors found in promotion packages. The data provide insights into common errors.

This chapter provides a description of existing processes for original appointment and promotion scrolls within OEPM. It then provides a depiction of error rates and common errors as captured in OEPM-generated data.

Process Descriptions

Scrolls are generated for two processes: original appointments of officers and promotions to higher grades. The scrolling processes further include federal recognition of officers in the Army National Guard and the Air National Guard.

Original Appointments

DoDI 1310.02 stipulates the categories of officers requiring original appointments. All officers on the active-duty list must have a regular appointment, and all officers on the reserve active-status list must have a reserve appointment. Original appointments are required for

> an individual entering a Military Service for the first time through any military accession program; a former officer returning to service; an enlisted member completing an officer program; an officer transferring between Military Services; an officer transferring between components within a Military Service; an individual, enlisted member, or officer appointed by warrant or commissioned as a warrant officer; or a warrant officer being appointed as a commissioned officer (DoDI 1310.02, 2015, p. 8).

This DoDI also outlines special circumstances requiring an original appointment. These special circumstances include Army officers transferring between basic and special branches, regular officers in the Navy transferring between the line and staff corps, and officers whose transfers result in a change in grade or service credit.

Original appointment scrolls vary in length. Some only include one name; others include thousands of names.[1] In FYs 2017 and 2018, OEPM processed 2,703 scrolls containing 99,362 individual names (Government Accountability Office [GAO], 2019).

Information Provided on the Scroll

DoDI 1310.02 stipulates the information required on the header of an original appointment scroll.[2] The scroll header must include the *person type*, which is a description of the officer's pre-appointment status. The three types of person are *individual* (a civilian with no prior military service), *enlisted member*, and *officer*. The appointment scroll must also indicate whether the appointment is *in* or *to* the specified grade. Indi-

---

1 The only upper limitation stipulated in DoDI 1320.04 is that scrolls should not be longer than 175 pages. If the scroll would be more than 175 pages if printed on one side only, the service is required to print the scroll front and back.

2 Figure 1.1 in Chapter One depicts the header template.

viduals, enlisted members, and officers can all be appointed *to* a grade if they do not currently hold the grade. An officer is appointed *in* the grade if already serving in that grade (for example, when transferring from the active component to the reserve component or between services). An incorrect use of *in* or *to* the grade results in an error, requiring a correction by the service or OEPM.

The inclusion of the person type and *in* or *to* the grade classification provides the services, OEPM, OSD, the White House, and the Senate with information regarding an officer's prior service. It also raises important considerations regarding other potentially necessary documentation. For example, use of the term *individual* indicates that the person being added to an original appointment scroll has no prior military experience or current military status. Most individuals are appointed to the grade of O-1; however, some individuals receive constructive credit and are appointed to a more senior grade (also known as lateral entry). The appointment scroll for an individual appointed to a more senior grade requires a supporting constructive credit worksheet. Including the term *individual* in a more senior grade appointment is useful because it alerts each reviewing office to the necessity of this supporting documentation. However, the extra information included in the scroll header also increases the potential for errors on the scroll.

Process

OEPM receives appointment packages from the military departments in two forms: (1) electronic documents and data uploaded or entered into OEPM's General and Flag Officer Decision Support System (DSS), the system used for appointment scroll management, and (2) a package of printed documents. The total package contains a forwarding memorandum from the submitting military department, the appointment scroll itself, the Senate text file (if Senate confirmation is required and there are more than three names on a scroll), and other supporting documentation (DoDI 1320.04, 2014, p. 57). If OEPM staff identify errors, they can either correct the error within OEPM or return the package to the originating military department for correction. OEPM is more likely to return a package for minor errors if a service consistently submits scrolling packages with similar errors.

Major errors (such as missing documentation) almost always require returning the appointment package to the service. OEPM keeps track of errors and whether those errors are addressed at OEPM or at their originating services.

Once the package is corrected for any errors identified at OEPM, it is forwarded to OGC for review. Since the appointment scroll is a legal document and is signed by either the Secretary of Defense or the President, OGC reviews the scrolls to ensure compliance and correctness. In some cases, OGC identifies an error not detected by OEPM. If an error is detected by OGC, the OGC returns the package to OEPM, which coordinates revisions or clarification on questions with the services. OEPM records the number and types of errors identified by OGC. Common concerns identified by OGC include whether an officer will promote before or after a transfer between components; incorrect name spellings, components, and grades; and verification of whether the constructive credit worksheets provided for lateral commissions are included in the appointment package.

After these reviews are complete and the package is free of errors, it is submitted to OUSD (P&R). If no errors are identified, OUSD (P&R) submits the scrolling package to the Executive Services Directorate of OSD's Washington Headquarters Services. The package is delivered to OSD for appointments made at that level or, for those requiring Presidential appointment and Senate confirmation, to the Office of the Deputy Secretary of Defense for forwarding to the White House. After receiving either a signed scroll from the Secretary of Defense or a Senate consent document, the Executive Services Directorate sends email notifications to the concerned military department and provides signed documents to OEPM for further distribution to the military departments.

OEPM updates the status of the package in DSS at various steps in the process. DSS currently only has limited automatic feedback mechanisms. Working within the limitations of the current DSS, OEPM staff have developed a request for information (RFI) form to inform the services about errors, questions, and missing documents. These RFIs include due dates for service response; OEPM staff report that these due dates have reduced service response time. The RFI document is uploaded to DSS, but DSS does not automatically alert service representatives regarding updates in the system. Service staff must manually check the system for potential returned packages. Once the service updates a DSS task, the service representative emails OEPM staff to alert them of the update. OEPM staff check for updates two or three times per day. The daily checks require a manual process in which staff refresh the DSS home screen to check for updated time stamps. Once RFIs are addressed, OEPM staff ensure that the revised files are correct and complete. They then forward the updated file and any clarifications to OGC.

Original Appointment Package Error Rates

OEPM began recording error rates and common reporting errors in September 2019. The office created the following categories of original appointment package:

1. *green packages* are correct and able to be processed
2. *yellow packages* raise questions regarding the accuracy of an element (such as the spelling of a name) but do not require sending the package back to the service
3. *red packages* have enough errors that the package must be returned to the service for correction.

OEPM categorizes inaccurate scrolling packages by the following types of error:

- contains a name spelling error
- incorrectly formatted
- includes a grade error
- includes a person type error
- includes a component error
- incorrect usage of *in* or *to*
- incorrect reference to the U.S. Code section
- incorrect header paragraph grammar
- multiple types of error.

Between September 2019 and February 2020, the majority of original appointment packages (221 out of 341, or 64.8 percent) were coded as green. Twenty-three (or 6.7 percent) were coded as yellow. Ninety-seven (or 28.4 percent) were coded as red and had to be returned to their respective services. Table 2.1 depicts the distribution of original appointment package errors by absolute number and percentage.

After OEPM addressed the errors through coordination with the services, they submitted the original appointment packages to OGC. OGC determined that 54 of the 341 scrolling packages still contained errors or required clarification.

The most common error for red packages was misspelled names, which were present in 11 of the 97 red appointment scrolls. Although these scrolls must be returned to their services to correct the spelling, the corrections can be made within a short time frame.

Other errors require more time to address, such as possible errors regarding the sequencing of an officer's transfer between components and pending promotions. These errors occur when an officer is included on a promotion scroll and a transfer scroll (typically from an active to a reserve appointment) at the same time and it is unclear which scroll will be processed first. If the promotion precedes the appointment, the scroll prepared for the component transfer appointment *in* the pre-promotion grade will be in error. Three of the 97 scrolls coded red in the OEPM data were flagged for this issue.

Original appointment scrolls for lateral commissions require a constructive credit worksheet to ensure that the individual meets the

Table 2.1
Original Appointments Package Error Categorization

Package Error Category	Number	Percentage
Green	221	64.8
Yellow	23	6.7
Red	97	28.4
Total	341	100.0

SOURCE: OEPM data, September 2019–February 2020.
NOTE: Because of rounding, percentages do not equal 100 percent exactly.

requirements for the assigned grade. In at least two of the 97 cases coded red, OGC returned an appointment package because of a lack of proper constructive credit documentation.

Effects of Errors on Processing Timelines

DoDI 1320.04 defines the OSD processing time as approximately 21 duty days. OEPM guidance to the services requires submission of original appointment packages at least two weeks in advance of any required action. OEPM aims to process all original appointments (including OGC review) within six working days. The data reveal that the modal length of time it takes for OEPM and OGC to process a clean original appointment package is one business day. However, some original appointment packages take much longer to process. The data do not specify whether the additional processing time is caused by extended time in OEPM or at the service level. However, based on OEPM's two-week requirement, the office's goal of processing appointments within six business days, and its modal processing time of one business day, it is reasonable to infer that original appointment packages that took longer than two weeks to process were returned to the services for rework.

Identifying and correcting errors affect the time it takes to process an original appointment scroll. OEPM provided processing time data for all officers in the grades of O-6 and below from 2015 through 2018—a total of 3,636 scroll entries.[3] The data include both the initial date that OEPM received the appointment package and the date that the package was coordinated by OGC. This timeline includes returning a package to the services for correction (if necessary).

The data indicate that original appointment processing time increased for all services between 2016 and 2018. Figure 2.1 depicts this trend.

These trends might be explained by a few factors. First, the number of errors could be increasing over time. However, the level of scrutiny applied to appointment packages might be increasing over

---

[3] The original data file included 4,066 scroll entries; however, because of a systematic flaw in entry updates for some 2015 and 2016 data, we did not include 430 of the entries.

Figure 2.1
Original Appointment Processing Times by Service (All Components)

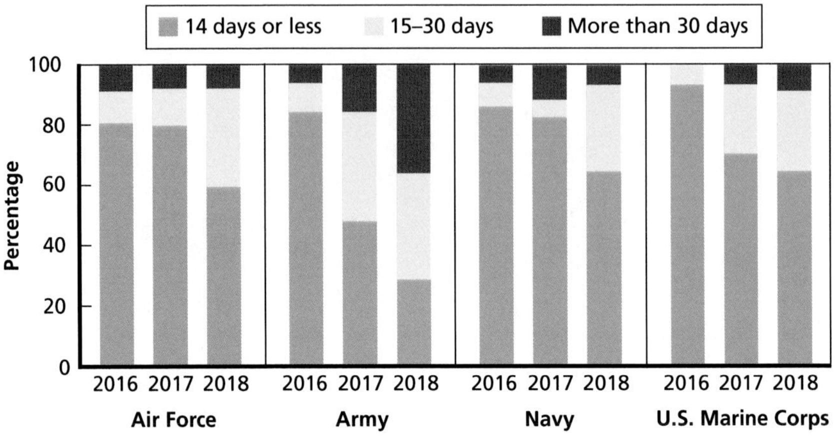

SOURCE: Data provided by OEPM.
NOTE: Available data did not permit ready differentiation by active or reserve component.

time, meaning that more errors are being caught, not that more errors exist. According to interviews, OEPM now is more likely to return a package to the service if it contains an error that the service has consistently repeated; previously, OEPM staff might have made the correction for the service. Turnover in the offices that are responsible for processing scrolls might lead to inefficiency; however, service-level data regarding turnover rates were not examined for this study.

Promotions

Promotion scroll packages are handled and routed in a manner similar to the original appointment scroll process. The package includes promotion-specific elements, such as the promotion board report and promotion list. As with original appointment packages, the services provide promotion packages to OEPM, where staff review the completeness and correctness of the packages. After any required corrections, the packages are reviewed by OGC, where more errors might be detected.

Promotion scrolls include those documenting federal recognition for National Guard promotions. Guard officers are promoted by the states through their governors, and these promotions must be federally recognized for the officer to receive the associated federal pay (National Guard Association of the United States, 2019). National Guard officers promoted to the grades of O-2 through O-5 are federally recognized by the Secretary of Defense; National Guard officers promoted to the grades of O-6 and above are federally recognized by the President and the Senate. For both categories, the scroll review process is the same within OEPM. In FY 2017 and FY 2018, OEPM processed 129 federal recognition scrolls containing 12,475 names (GAO, 2019).

Information Provided on the Scroll

Promotion scrolls provide the same information as original appointment scrolls, including the person type, whether the person is being appointed *in* or *to* the grade classification, and the title specification.

Promotion Package Error Rates

OEPM has recorded error rates for promotion packages since 2010. The color-coding scheme for promotion scroll errors is slightly different from the color-coding scheme applied to original appointment errors. Promotion packages are coded in the following ways:

1. *green packages* are correct and able to be processed
2. *yellow packages* contain a minor error that OEPM is able to correct or contain an advisory note that the military department needs to be concerned with for the next package
3. *red packages* contain an error that requires OEPM to return the file to the service for correction; red packages are also defined as any package in which OEPM has to correct scrolls, Senate text files, or summary sheets.

Figures 2.2 through 2.5 depict trends across each of the services and components. The figures include a comparison of both the absolute numbers of files categorized as green, yellow, or red and the percentage of files coded as green (no corrections required).

Figure 2.2
Reported Error Rates for Promotion Packages, Army, 2010–2019

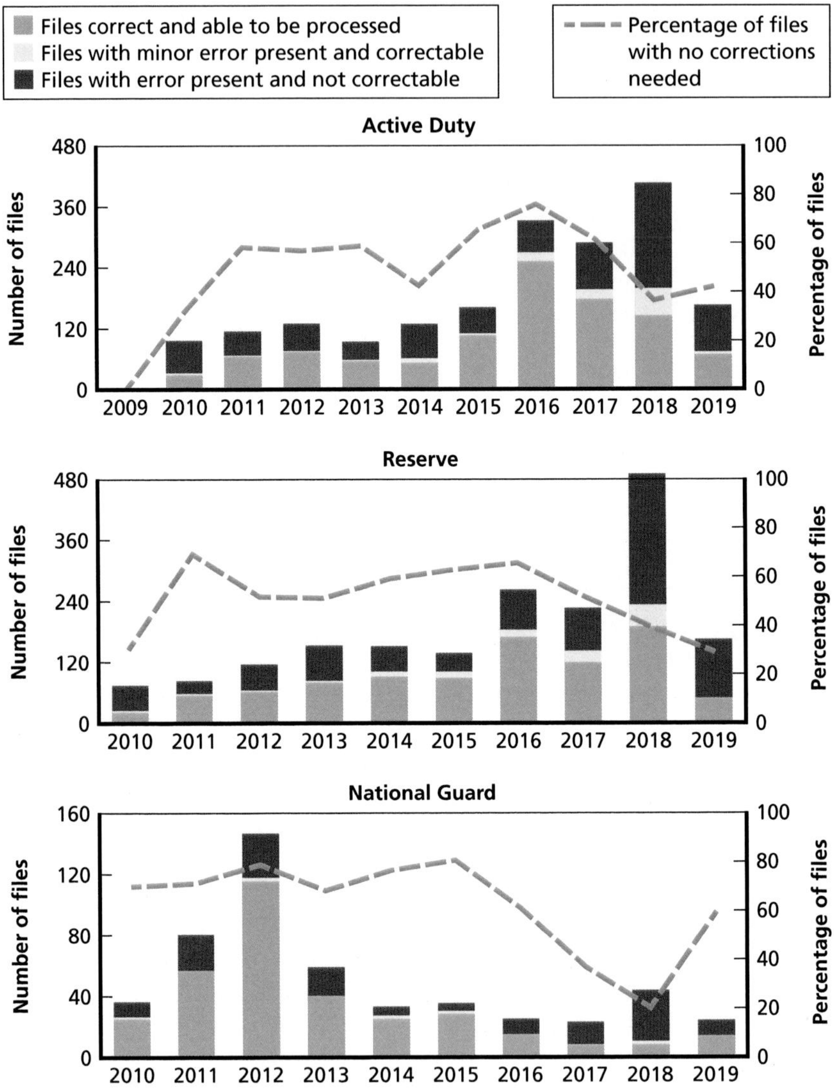

SOURCE: Data provided by OEPM.

Figure 2.3
Reported Error Rates for Promotion Packages, Air Force, 2010–2019

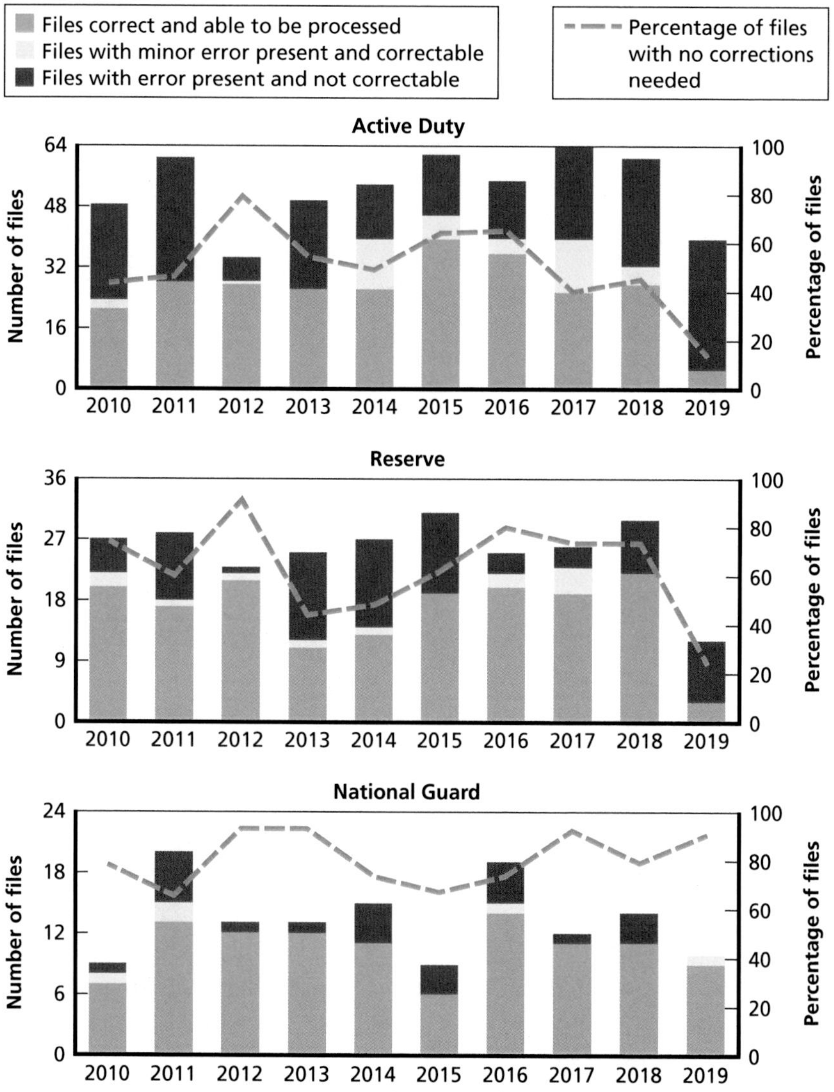

SOURCE: Data provided by OEPM.

Figure 2.4
Reported Error Rates for Promotion Packages, Navy, 2010–2019

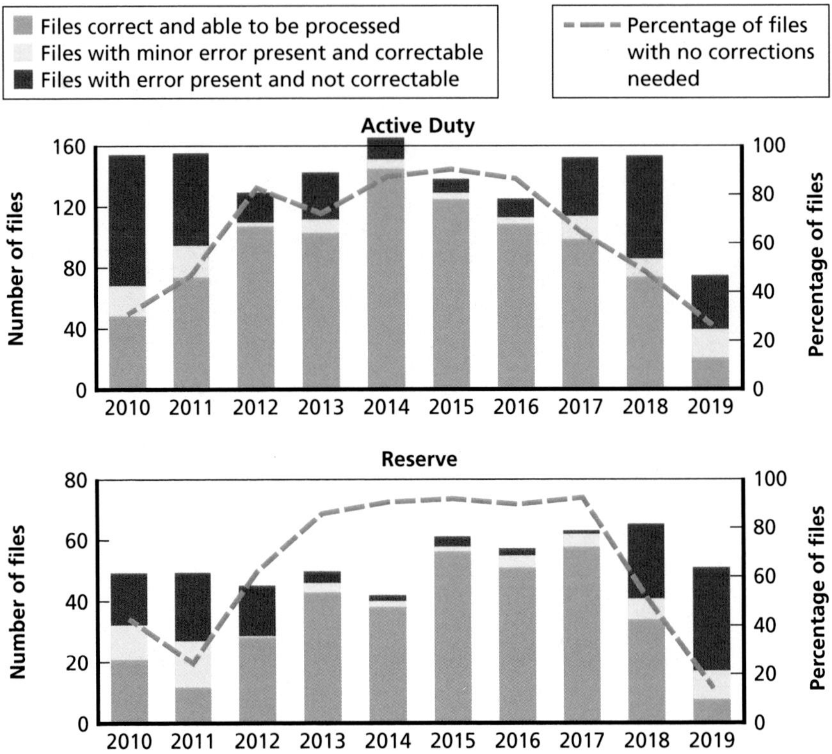

SOURCE: Data provided by OEPM.

Accuracy rates have decreased since 2016 for every service and component, with the exceptions of the Navy Reserve (where accuracy rates have decreased since 2017) and the Air National Guard, the active-duty Army, and the Army National Guard (all of which improved between 2018 and 2019). The potential underlying explanations for increased error rates in promotion packages are similar to those for original appointments packages. First, the raw number of errors might be increasing over time. In addition, the level of scrutiny applied to promotion packages might be increasing over time, meaning that more errors are being identified for correction. Just as with original appoint-

Figure 2.5
Reported Error Rates for Promotion Packages, Marine Corps, 2010–2019

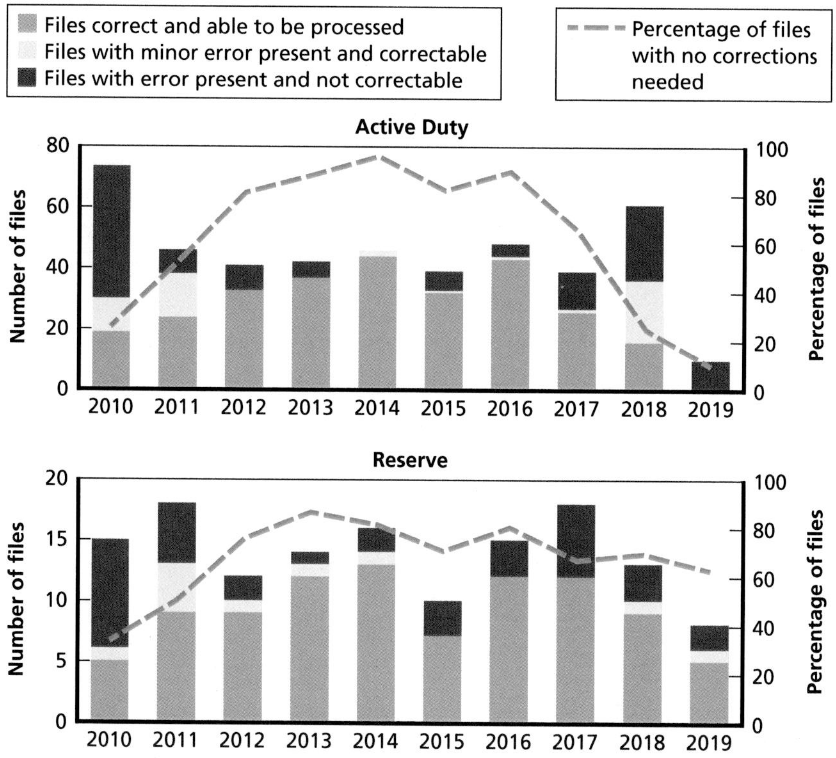

SOURCE: Data provided by OEPM.

ment packages, OEPM is more likely to return a promotion package to the service if it contains errors that the service tends to repeat.

Data System Limitations

As mentioned above, DSS has limitations that affect OEPM efficiency in processing scroll packages. First, DSS is a package-tracking system; DSS users cannot search DSS by the names of the individuals on the scrolls. Appointment scrolls are uploaded to DSS in the PDF file format and saved under the name of the first officer on the scroll. The actual scrolls can include a number of names ranging from one to thousands. If OEPM staff need to locate an officer for verification purposes, they cannot run a simple search function for the individual officer's name; instead, they must be able to link that officer's name to the name of the first officer listed on the scroll to locate the correct document.

DSS also provides limited accountability to its users. Service staff who use DSS view landing pages that provide limited information regarding the current status of submitted appointment and promotion packages. In addition, the landing pages do not provide information regarding current error rates or types of errors. A more automated DSS could provide real-time feedback to the services on their respective landing pages. Such information could modify service behavior, decreasing the number of appointment or promotion packages submitted with errors or missing information.

Information Format

As prescribed in DoDI 1320.04, information is provided to OEPM in both digital and paper formats. The appointment package is provided in hard copy for action within OSD. Electronic documents are provided so that OEPM staff can edit them (if necessary); they are also provided in the Senate text file for scrolls with three or more names for those scrolls requiring Senate confirmation. The services are responsible for providing scrolls printed on a specified type of paper. The services are also responsible for uploading a Word version of a scroll to DSS. The services must further provide electronic files in ASCII (.txt) format for Senate text files for O-7 and O-8 promotion and for O-6 and below promotions that require Senate confirmation.

Currently, the services provide both printed and digital copies of scrolls to OEPM at the point of initial appointment or promotion submission. Although this process is ideal if the package is complete and correct, it has the effect of multiplying service workloads when corrections are required because of the need to reprint packages. A more efficient approach would allow printing at the last possible stage in the process.

Either an Excel-based scroll list worksheet or comparable fields in an enhanced DSS could be used as the source for printing at a later stage.[4]

Summary

Overall, OEPM has identified an increasing rate of errors in both original appointment scroll and promotion scroll package submissions. The increase is likely the result of both the raw number of errors generated by the services and increased levels of scrutiny applied to errors in the scrolling packages. Error correction, in turn, increases processing times.

Existing OEPM data systems hamper efficiency because staff need to manually update documents and have limited search capability. Upgrades to DSS could reduce administrative burdens on OEPM staff and facilitate error correction. As we discuss in Chapter Five, an enhanced DSS also could prevent errors from being introduced into the process.

---

4 An example of an Excel-based scroll list worksheet is provided in Appendix C.

CHAPTER THREE

Military Department Processes

Each of the military departments has its own distinct approach to creating and managing scroll packages. Within a department, processes differ by purpose (original appointment versus promotion), component (active, reserve, National Guard), source of commission, and grade (general and flag officers versus lower ranks). These processes are described in this chapter and illustrated using process maps (see Appendix B for these maps).

Two main issues emerged in our review of military department processes. First, decentralized processing (many activities playing a role in constructing scrolls) makes quality assurance more difficult. It engages many more activities, each requiring staff trained in the nuances of the scrolling process. Because military staff change positions at regular intervals, maintaining the required level of training is challenging. Second, automation can significantly enhance error-trapping in the preparation of scrolls. Unfortunately, we found the automation to be limited and uneven.

In the following sections, we describe key characteristics of each military service's scrolling processes. The Army treatment is lengthier than the others in its description of challenges commonly faced by all of the services.

Army

Scrolling processes in the Army are centralized at two locations: Army Human Resources Command (HRC) processes O-6 and below scrolls, and Headquarters, Department of the Army (HQDA) General Officer Management Office processes general officer scrolls. Army HRC is responsible for original appointment and promotion scrolls for both active and reserve component officers, while HQDA General Officer Management Office has responsibility for general officer promotions and selections across components. In this section, we briefly describe the scrolling processes for the Army, present some key differences in scrolling requirements between the active and reserve components, and identify areas in which current scrolling requirements create challenges for the Army.

Process Description

The Reserve Personnel Management Directorate, Officer Accessions Branch (OAB) at Army HRC manages the creation of all original appointment scrolls. The process begins when the division receives a submission for an appointment scroll from one of the 13 sources of commission:

- U.S. Military Academy
- U.S. Army Cadet Command/Reserve Officers' Training Corps (ROTC)
- U.S. Army Recruiting Command
- National Guard (Federal Recognition)
- Reserve of the Army (RC)
- Officer Candidate School (OCS)
- Call to Active Duty (CAD)/Inter-Service Transfer
- Education Delay Program
- Warrant Officer Candidate School
- Cyber Command
- Health Services Department (Specialty Branch)
- Chaplain Corps (Specialty Branch)
- Judge Advocate General Corps (Specialty Branch).

The data package submitted to Army HRC contains names in a spreadsheet and documentation that verifies the names in the spreadsheet. OAB reviews this data package for appropriate source documentation (e.g., birth certificates, marriage certificates, the DA4187 [Personnel Action] form completed during in-processing). If source documentation is incomplete, processors return the data package to the appropriate source to address the incomplete submission. Once OAB confirms this documentation, the Soldier Management System (SMS) verifies administrative information (i.e., name, Social Security number [SSN], rank) for individuals in the scroll package. Personnel use SMS to check across several systems of record to verify this administrative information and check for derogatory information. The systems of record used depend on the component; we discuss them in the Electronic Platforms portion of this section. In addition, OAB uses SMS and the Access database to check for any duplicate scrolls in the system.

Following checks for derogatory information and duplicity, the scroll list is loaded into SMS via a .csv file; an in-house tool produces the scroll and the accompanying action memorandum (developed in Word). The scroll and memorandum are forwarded to Army G-1, Directorate of Manpower and Personnel Management (DMPM). DMPM quality-checks the scroll to verify administrative information, statute citations, and supporting documentation; it returns the scroll package to the Officer Accessions Division if possible errors are found. Otherwise, DMPM, Accessions Division Chief, signs the action memorandum. DMPM also uploads the scroll package into the OEPM DSS and gives a hard copy to OEPM at this point. DMPM monitors DSS for any errors in scroll packages and scroll package approval.

The process for promotion scrolls is largely the same as the process for original appointment scrolls, except that this process is handled by the Officer Promotions Division at Army HRC. Once a promotion board adjourns or a Federal Recognition packet is received, Army HRC constructs the scrolls (typically six months before their anticipated release). The scroll files are constructed in Excel and then formatted in the proper Word template. Army HRC then prepares the action memo and submits the scroll and action memo to DMPM. At this point, the promotion package follows the same process as the original appointment package.

Electronic Platforms

The Army handles appointment scrolls in a centralized manner, and the creation and checks of scroll packages are largely the same among Army components. However, the components use different systems of record to verify information. The Interactive Personnel Electronic Records Management System (iPERMS) and the Total Officer Personnel Management Information System (TOPMIS) serve as systems of record for active-duty soldiers. The Army Reserve uses the Regional Level Application Software (RLAS), whereas the Army National Guard uses the Standard Installation/Division Personnel Reporting System (SIDPERS). Personnel who process scrolls for the Army also use the Army Military Human Resource Record when evaluating personnel for possible derogatory information.

All components of the Army are planned to transition to the Integrated Personnel and Pay System–Army (IPPS-A), which will subsume these systems of record and should eliminate the need for proficiency across a variety of electronic platforms when processing scrolls.

Unique Factors

In accordance with 10 U.S.C. §7064 and §7153, active component original appointments and promotions require that service members being assigned to basic branches (e.g., Infantry, Engineer, Field Artillery, Armor) be on different scrolls than those being assigned to special branches (e.g., Judge Advocate General Corps, Medical Corps, Chaplain Corps). Transfers to and from basic and special branches and between special branches require rescrolling. The Army should consider a legislative proposal that would eliminate the need to rescroll officers transitioning between basic and specialty branches.

In addition, there are some differences between active component and RC appointment scrolls. RC appointment scrolls are not differentiated for basic and special branches. As with all services, only RC scrolls for the rank of colonel and above require Senate confirmation (Regular Army [RA] appointment scrolls for the rank of major and above require Senate confirmation).

Other Concerns

Several aspects of scroll processing cause an increased burden on Army staff or affect units or service members.

Delays Following Office of Secretary of Defense and Office of General Counsel Review

OGC review sometimes results in requests for information for individuals on a proposed scroll. According to Army personnel, many of these requests require a hands-on approach and necessitate coordination with multiple agencies to get a satisfactory answer. For example, OGC might have a question regarding an officer who is simultaneously transferring between components and awaiting placement on a promotion scroll. In those cases, OGC could raise questions regarding the sequencing of the transfer and the promotion to determine whether the officer is being transferred at the appropriate grade. Although Army HRC keeps a listing of all instances of these requests from OGC, there is no standard response because the requests can raise a variety of issues. The other services report similar problems.

Regular Army to Reserve Component Transitions

There is no automated system to alert Army HRC that a service member needs to receive a scroll for a different component. Rather, the separating service member must signal an intention to affiliate with a reserve component. It is not uncommon for a service member separating from active duty to make this decision at a point very late in their transition process. However, the service member still must receive an approved appointment scroll for the RC prior to their separation date.

There are several situations in which Army HRC sees problematic RA to RC transitions. (Representatives from the other services indicate similar challenges.) The following scenarios are regularly encountered during transitions from the RA to the RC:

- **Scenario 1: An RA soldier transitioning to the RC does not have an RC appointment scroll at the current rank.** The service member must extend active-duty service until their RC scroll is confirmed. This scenario has many potential side effects. Because the service member already has an approved separation date, they might also have an agreed-upon civilian job start date and have shipped their household goods. An extension on active duty could delay a civilian job start, effectively placing that job opportunity at risk. In addition, dependents might already have relocated to the new job location, resulting in a lack of family continuity and an additional financial burden.

- **Scenario 2: An RA soldier transitioning to the RC does not have an RC appointment scroll at the current rank and has been discharged into civilian status.** In this scenario, the service member has decided to serve in the RC during the separation process—at which point it is too late to process a scroll. Although the service member avoids the disruption to their transition as experienced in Scenario 1, the soldier must apply for reappointment to the RC and cannot drill with their RC unit—potentially creating a risk for unit readiness. Reappointment into the reserve component can only take place after confirmation of an RC appointment scroll. In addition to being unable to drill with their reserve unit, the service member incurs a break in service in this scenario. Breaks in service can have numerous adverse effects. A break in service can change the service member's year group, affecting the timing of consideration for future promotion boards. Other adverse effects might include disruption in medical and dental benefits for dependents or a break in continuity of care for a current medical condition.
- **Scenario 3: An RA service member is released from active duty and transitions to the RC without an RC appointment scroll.** In this scenario, the service member is an erroneous accession to the RC. A service member later identified as an erroneous accession risks incurring debt, losing service time, and losing promotion opportunity for all duty served between their time of separation from active duty and approval of an RC appointment scroll.

Service members selected for promotion after receipt of an approved separation date and before RC appointment further exacerbate the effects of each of these scenarios. Once promoted in the RA, the service member must be rescrolled for the reserve component at the higher rank. Army HRC personnel shared that this often adds eight to 12 weeks to the transition process.

Reserve Component to Regular Army Transitions via the Call to Active Duty Program

Once Army HRC approves a CAD packet, an RC service member must have an approved RA appointment scroll before serving on active duty. Army HRC personnel who process scrolls shared that there is rarely sufficient time between notification of an approved CAD action and the date to report to active duty to process a scroll for the service member. Typically, the soldier must extend their reserve status while waiting for the RA appointment scroll when participating in the CAD program. Reserve component service members transitioning to active duty via CAD also face similar challenges to active duty service members transitioning to the reserve component when the service member experiences a promotion during the transition period. The following scenarios highlight this challenge for reserve component service members:

- **Scenario 1: An RC service member with an RA scroll for their current rank receives an RC promotion after production of the CAD appointment order; the service member has not yet reported to their RA unit.** In this case, OAB must revoke the service member's order to active duty to avoid an erroneous accession. The wait period for the appointment scroll to the next higher grade is typically six to 12 months. The RC service member might already have terminated their civilian employment in anticipation of assignment on active duty, and this revocation might affect the service member's housing (a service member might have ended a lease in anticipation of moving to base housing). The service member's prospective RA unit also suffers because it loses the expected RC service member, potentially affecting unit readiness.
- **Scenario 2: An RC service member receives an RC promotion after production of the CAD appointment order; the service member already has reported to their RA unit.** In this case, the

service member must report to their active-duty position at the lower grade despite the promotion because there is no appointment scroll in the higher grade for the RA. OAB must manage this case with a ratification appointment scroll, a process which can take six to 12 months.

It is more difficult to recommend solutions for the issues associated with CAD. Initiating a scroll for the officer once Army HRC receives the CAD packet, instead of after CAD packet approval, might reduce delays. However, we have no data on CAD packet processing times that would allow us to examine whether such a practice would mitigate the negative outcomes associated with CAD scrolling requirements. The Army should consider capturing the processing times for CAD packets for future study.

Air Force

Air Force processes appear to be somewhat less centralized than those of the Army but more so than those of the Navy. The Air Force is notable in that it has progressed further than the other services in automating its original appointment scrolling process.

Process Description

Air Force scrolls originate from a wide variety of sources, depending on their purpose (original appointment or promotion), component, grade level, occupation, and service member accession source. Scroll packages follow various routes through processing activities, depending on their source. The process begins when Officer Accessions receives a submission for an appointment scroll from one of the following commissioning sources:

- Air Force Recruiting Service
- Air Force Personnel Center
- Air Reserve Personnel Center
- National Guard Bureau

- Air National Guard Support Center
- State National Guard headquarters
- Air Force Directorate of Military Force Management Policy
- Air Force General Officer Management Office
- Chief of Air Force Reserve.

Original appointment scrolling for all Air Force components is partially centralized. Although nominations originate from various sources in each component, all components place their nominees in a standardized Excel file format (see Appendix C) that incorporates some data validation rules. Using either uploads of the Excel files or single-name data inputs, all nominees are recorded in a scrolling module within the Air Force Recruiting Information Support System (AFRISS). AFRISS provides additional data validation rules (see Appendix D) and a medium for storing images of supporting documentation. For example, by policy, copies of nominees' Social Security cards are uploaded as a part of each scroll package in AFRISS. A single Air Force processing point for all components (the Air Force Accessions and Training Management Division) invokes a programmed process to print scrolls from the data uploaded to AFRISS. This office assembles the appointment packages, obtains the required coordinations and signatures, uploads material to DSS, and submits printed packages to OEPM.

Promotion scroll processing is less centralized. For O-6 and below promotions, each component prepares and submits its own packages. For general officer promotions to grades O-7 and O-8, which are based on selection or federal recognition boards, packages are prepared, coordinated, and submitted by the Air Force General Officer Management Office for active-duty promotions and Air National Guard federal recognition and by the Air Force Reserve Senior Leader Management Office for Air Force Reserve promotions.

Air Force officials indicate that, on large scrolls, a sample is checked for issues that require correction. If issues are found in the sample, a more complete check is conducted.

Active-to-reserve and reserve-to-active transfer issues are similar to those discussed earlier for Army transitions.

Electronic Platforms

Platforms used in scroll management and production include AFRISS, the Air Force Military Personnel Data System, the Air Force Promotion System (used for promotion board support and results reporting), and various senior leader management systems.

Unique Factors

The automation, error-checking, and electronic coordination features built into the Air Force's AFRISS-based system for appointment scrolls can serve as a model for other departments seeking to more fully automate their processes. Since implementation of this system in 2019, the Air Force error rate for original appointments has fallen to a level that is significantly less than that of the other services.

Other Concerns

The Air Force seems to have automated its processes to the extent possible, given that its final products delivered to OSD must include key elements in paper formats. Additional automation would require DSS to provide an electronic interface between OSD and the services at an individual officer level.

Navy

The Navy system for generating and tracking original appointments is more distributed than the other services. The distributed responsibility can lead to miscommunication between OEPM and the Navy regarding scrolling issues because there are 14 points of contact for Navy scrolling issues (compared with one point of contact in the Army and the Air Force). The Navy maintains scrolling contacts in Washington, D.C., and at Naval Support Activity Mid-South (Millington).

Process Description

The process begins when the Navy Recruiting Command or Naval Personnel Command receives a submission for an appointment scroll from one of the following sources of commission:

- U.S. Naval Academy
- Naval ROTC
- Naval Nuclear Propulsion Officer Candidate Program
- Naval Civil Engineer Collegiate Program
- Health Professions Scholarship Program
- Chaplain Candidate Program
- Officer Candidate School
- Officer Development School.

The scrolling process in the Navy generally starts in two places: Navy Recruiting Command (NRC) and Navy Personnel Command (NPC). At NRC, scrolls are processed on a monthly schedule. Program managers check information before submitting to the NRC scrolling office, at which point program managers upload the packets to a SharePoint server and produce an electronic memorandum from the signature authority and the scroll. These electronic files are then forwarded to the NRC's Washington liaison; the liaison reviews them and then downloads and prints the files, puts the scrolls on proper paper and letterhead, and delivers the printed scrolls to OEPM.

There are several branches within NPC that handle scrolling processes. The Board Administration Branch (PERS-804) acts as a liaison between NPC and Navy Chief of Personnel, the Judge Advocate General's Corps, Chief of Naval Operations, and the Secretary of the Navy regarding appointment scrolls and provides quality assurance to all nomination and appointment scrolls. The Officer Performance and Separations Branch (PERS-834)

> prepares and provides monthly inputs to the Active to Reserve Duty scrolls to [the Secretary of Defense] requiring approval/disapproval of officer appointments in the [U.S. Navy Reserve] (original appointments) including applicant transferring to the Navy from other armed services (inter-service appointment), favorable separations and officer whom twice fail to select for promotion (Navy Personnel Command Instruction 5400.1A, 2015).

Transitions between the active and reserve scrolls are managed by separate offices within NPC. Officers transitioning from the active scroll to the reserve scroll must first submit a request to resign from the active scroll to the NPC Career Transition Office at least nine months prior to their intended date of separation. Once the officer's resignation is processed with the NPC Career Transition Office, the Joint Officer Management (PERS-451) submits the officer's name for the reserve scroll (Naval Personnel Command Career Transition Office, undated). Officers who do not initially request a reserve appointment upon separation from active duty may request a reserve appointment within three years after their separation through the Reserve Personnel Administrative Branch (PERS-91) (Navy Personnel Command Manual 1131-040, 2013).

The Reserve Officer Recall and Full Time Support Redesignation Branch (PERS-923) submits and tracks commissioning scroll requests for reserve officers volunteering for transition to the active component for a "temporary and definite" period, who are augmenting the active component, or who are converting to a full-time support position.

The current distributed system was created as a corrective to the previous system, in which all appointments and promotions were processed through the Navy Chief of Personnel's office. Although the process ensured one central point of contact between the Navy and OEPM, the level of file review created a bottleneck, extending the amount of processing time internal to the Navy. Within the current system, Navy staff are uncertain about the correct point of contact for OEPM when questions arise regarding a specific scroll. One solution might be to have a centralized system with a single authority to serve as a final quality check and as the single point of contact between Navy and OEPM. While we were conducting this study, the Navy was in the midst of considering ways to increase efficiency by establishing a single-point-of-contact system.

Electronic Platforms

The Navy uses three primary electronic platforms in its scrolling processes: the Personalized Recruiting for Immediate and Delayed Enlistment Modernization (PRIDE), a SharePoint system, and Excel files. All information from NRC initially comes through PRIDE, the Navy recruitment system. Any errors entered into PRIDE could carry through to later steps. Program managers reformat the information from PRIDE into Excel files on SharePoint, from which the program managers create both digital and printed copies of appointment scrolls. Program managers then upload the packets into the Navy tasker system and provide the requisite files to OEPM through DSS.

Unique Factors

Within the Navy, officers are assigned as either line officers (unrestricted line or restricted line) or staff corps officers. Line officers serve in operational command positions; staff officers serve in combat support positions. DoDI 1310.02, conforming to 10 U.S.C. §8132, specifies that a regular officer in a grade not above lieutenant commander transferring from the line to the staff corps or from the staff corps to the line requires a new original appointment. This results in additional Navy scrolls not required in other services.

Other Concerns

The current policy that scrolls need to be downloaded and put on proper letterhead seems outdated to some Navy staff, especially because almost everything else operates through PDF files. In addition, Navy service representatives were concerned about potential expectations that a Marine Corps process might be required within the Department of the Navy. In the Marine Corps, individuals transitioning from active duty to the reserve components with remaining service obligations are automatically scrolled 180 days prior to their transition. Navy service representatives expressed a concern that a similar process could create a lot of rework and make it difficult to accommodate other circumstances (e.g., if someone chooses to not go to a reserve component immediately).

Marine Corps

The Marine Corps assesses fewer officers on an annual basis and manages a smaller officer corps than the other services, enabling greater centralization. The Marine Corps scrolling process is centralized through the Marine Corps Recruiting Command (MCRC) Officer Appointment section. Marine Corps officers commission through Naval ROTC programs, the Naval Academy, or through OCS (referred to in the Marine Corps as Platoon Leaders Course [PLC]).[1] Officers in the other services are assigned to a career field prior to commissioning, but Marine Corps officers are commissioned to the service and then attend the Basic School, where their performance factors into career field assignments and assignment of first duty station. Original appointment scrolls must be submitted in a timely manner to facilitate assignments to Basic School and broader career management.

Process Description

The Marine Corps appointment system is highly centralized through the MCRC's Officer Appointments section. Officer Selection Teams (regionally aligned teams located at Officer Selection Stations across the United States) are required to submit requests for appointment (RFAs) to the Officer Appointments Section no later than 120 days before the scheduled commissioning date (Marine Corps Recruiting Command Officer Commissioning Manual, 2016, p. 1-3). The Marine Corps uses an RFA checklist (attached as a cover sheet) outlining the required materials within the file, including those materials required for the officer's name to be added to the original appointment scroll. The Officer Appointments Section returns a packet without action if the Officer Selection Team submits an incomplete RFA packet, potentially resulting in the delay of an officer's commissioning and their placement in a Basic School class.

Candidate materials for individuals commissioning in the Marine Corps through Navy ROTC and Services academies are submitted to the MCRC's Officer Appointments section between one year and 120 days prior to commissioning date. The Marine Corps liaison officer at the Naval Academy submits all materials for service academy

---

[1] Marine Corps PLC differs in structure from the other services' OCS programs. Officer candidates either attend summer training for six weeks following their freshman or sophomore years of college and six weeks following their junior year of college or attend for ten weeks following their junior year of college. Having completed the required training, PLC candidates then return to their university and are commissioned upon graduation.

commissions. Marine officer instructors submit materials for Navy ROTC graduates commissioning in the Marine Corps. Officer selection officers submit materials for candidates commissioning through the PLC.

Marine Corps districts provide their higher headquarters (regional commands) and MCRC with a monthly report identifying all candidates scheduled to commission in the following six months, providing multiple layers of accountability to ensure that appointment materials are submitted to OEPM in advance of an officer's commissioning. The Marine Corps plans for scrolls to take 45 to 60 days for final approval and submits scrolls to OEPM on a quarterly basis to ensure that all scrolls are processed before the scheduled commissioning date (Marine Corps Recruiting Command Officer Commissioning Manual, 2016, p. 21-3).

Electronic Platforms

The Marine Corps tracks the status of RFA submissions through the Marine Corps Recruiting Information Support System (MCRISS). MCRISS provides a digitized platform through which common processes (including RFAs) are automated to the greatest extent possible internal to the Marine Corps. However, MCRISS is not interoperable with DSS; therefore, RFAs submitted through MCRISS must then be formatted for DSS and printed scroll copies. The Marine Corps also uses the MCRC Share Portal to communicate information required by the Marine Corps for commissioning, including physical fitness test results and height and weight measurements, although this information is not required within the RFA.

Unique Factors

Platoon Leaders Course Law Commissions

The Marine Corps provides an option for candidates in law school to commission through the PLC Law program. Because candidates attending this program already possess a bachelor's degree, they commission immediately upon OCS graduation. By contrast, candidates completing traditional PLC do not commission until the date of the college graduation. PLC Law candidates receive their initial appointment to the Marine Corps Reserve and are placed on the Individual Ready Reserve while they complete law school. Upon law school graduation, PLC Law officers are assigned to active duty within the Marine Corps Judge Advocate General Corps. As is the process for traditional PLC graduates, PLC Law candidates' RFAs are submitted no less than 120 days prior to commissioning. Because PLC is a ten-week (70-day) course, original appointment packages for PLC Law candidates must be submitted well before PLC Law candidates begin their training to commission upon PLC graduation.

Transitions from the Active Component to the Reserve Component

The Marine Corps holds a career designation board (CDB) for all junior officers. To be eligible for the CDB, officers must have 540 days of observable operational time after graduating from their Military Occupational Specialty school before promotion to O-3. The purpose of the board is to identify the best-qualified Marine Corps officers for continued active-duty service. If an officer is not selected by the CDB, the officer is able to continue in the reserve component. Those officers transitioning to the reserve component with a remaining military service obligation (with an end of obligated service date later than their end of active service date) are required to be added to transition scrolls (Marine Administrative Message 080/11, 2011). The Marine Corps' Reserve Affairs division automatically screens and processes these officers for a reserve appointment. If an active-duty officer is not selected for continued active service by the CDB but has finished their obligated service, the officer must actively apply for a reserve commission. Transition scrolls are prepared once per month.

The Marine Corps is attempting to reduce the rework for officers who are transferring components and are expected to be placed on the promotion scrolls by providing two original appointment scrolls to OEPM: one in the service member's current grade and one in the service member's promotion grade. The Marine Corps limits dual-scroll submission to officers with a potential date of promotion and component transfer within four months of the scroll submission. With the exception of the appointment grades, the scrolls must contain the same information and list of names. This process allows OEPM to perform the requisite checks ahead of time and prevents last-minute changes to scrolls. However, as reported by OEPM, the Secretary of Defense's office is not a proponent of all services using this process.

Cross-Cutting Issues

Intercomponent Transfers

A persisting challenge across all services is the transfer of officers from the active component to the reserve component. Intercomponent transfers often take longer to process, particularly in cases where officers might be awaiting both an original appointment scroll (to the reserve component) and a promotion scroll.

Although precise data regarding the number of annual cross-component transfers were unavailable, the Army, Air Force, and Navy were able to report the approximate proportion of transfers between components during 2017–2018 to the GAO, as depicted in Table 3.1. The Marine Corps "did not provide a similar estimate but said that scrolls for transfers between components represent a large part of their workload" (GAO, 2019, p. 26).

Lack of Data System Interoperability

Another persistent challenge for all of the services is the lack of data systems that are interoperable with DSS. Each of the services has developed workarounds, combining recruitment software with commercial off-the-shelf technology, including SharePoint and Excel. The

Table 3.1
Approximate Proportion of Cross-Component Transfers

Service	Approximate Proportion of Cross-Component Transfers as a Percentage of Total Appointment Scrolls
Army	30 percent
Air Force	33 percent
Navy	25 percent

SOURCE: GAO, 2019, p. 26.

Air Force's automation of the process to the extent possible through AFRISS provides a potential example for all services to follow.

Appointments Related to Medical Education

Officers enrolled in the Health Sciences Educational Program attend medical school at the Uniformed Services University of Health Sciences (USUHS). Some officers attend USUHS directly after undergraduate education; others might attend after previously serving as a commissioned officer.

While attending USUHS, all officers are placed on an original appointment scroll to the grade of O-1 (even if they previously served as a commissioned officer at a higher grade). The service is responsible for submitting officer names on an original appointment scroll. USUHS advises services to submit Health Sciences Educational Program officer scrolls by February of the year that the officer will be assigned to USUHS. Upon graduation from USUHS, officers are promoted to the grade of O-3 by their respective service.

Some officers might desire to transfer from their original service to another service upon graduating from USUHS. In those cases, the officer must apply for a service transfer through their original service to the Board of Review for Interservice Transfer at USUHS. If this transfer is approved, the board will forward the application to the officer's original service. The original service initiates an interservice transfer scroll to remove the officer from the original scroll and place them on the new service scroll.

Foreseen Versus Unforeseen Last-Minute Packages

DoDI 1320.04 defines the OSD processing time as approximately 21 duty days. OEPM data show that between September 2019 and February 2020, 21 percent of all original appointment packages (71 of 341) were submitted with less than two weeks between submission and service requirements for action. Late submissions strain OEPM staff by magnifying the effort required to complete the appointments by the desired date.

Last-minute packages could be the result of unforeseen circumstances. However, the services should work to mitigate avoidable challenges with proper planning.

Avoidable Challenges

Interviews with OEPM and service representatives indicate that officers transitioning from the active component to the reserve component are the most common cause of last-minute packages. The issue arises when officers leaving the active component decide to transition to the reserve component at a late point in the process of leaving active duty. Officers must be added to the reserve scroll, a process that might take up to 180 days. The services want to retain the skills and experience of these officers, and, therefore, they are willing to submit last-minute packages to OEPM. These last-minute packages cause stress for both the service and OEPM systems. Alternatively, the officer might not be added to the reserve scroll in time to avoid a break in service, affecting their assignments and benefits.

The services can reduce the number of last-minute packages by better educating officers on the transfer process and the time required. Officers might not know of the requirement to rescroll to the reserve component until they are too far in their transition out of the active component. Officers are educated about the opportunity to transition to the reserve component during the Transition Assistance Program (TAP), a series of trainings intended to educate service members on health care, employment, education, and reserve opportunities. Traditionally, service members attend these trainings at a late stage in their transition process. However, recent updates to TAP require that individuals begin the process no less than 365 days prior to their anticipated separation (DoD, 2019). The new TAP structure and timeline presents an opportunity for the services to educate separating officers on the timeline required to transition to the reserve component.

OEPM also reported occasional original appointment oversights for entire ROTC battalions or OCS classes. Commissioning ceremonies are planned in advance for these groups, and they typically involve several new officers commissioning. When such oversights are identified at the last minute, the specific service and OEPM work together to ensure that the original appointments are processed, if possible. However, those cases strain OEPM and service resources. Proper enforcement of scrolling requirements by service cadet commands (including the U.S. Army Cadet Command, the Naval Service Training Command, and the Air Training Command) could prevent these problems from occurring.

Unforeseen Circumstances

Proper planning and oversight by the services could reduce the number of last-minute packages, but unforeseen circumstances might still arise. One member of service staff reported a case in which an active-duty officer decided to run for a seat in the U.S. House of Representatives and had to submit candidacy documentation in less than a week. Under DoD Directive 1344.10 (2008), active-duty officers are limited in their ability to fundraise, solicit votes, participate in partisan activities, or actively campaign. To retain a commission as a military officer, the officer had to transfer to a reserve component, requiring a short-notice reserve appointment scroll. The scroll was processed in one day.

Key Findings

The services vary in the degree to which the appointment and promotion scrolling processes are centralized. The Army and Marine Corps processes are highly centralized within one office, the Navy process is decentralized across several offices, and the Air Force process is decentralized but managed through a robust database system.

All of the services suffer from a lack of interoperability between their data systems and DSS. Each service has created workarounds, combining electronic platforms to track individual officer information and scroll processing. Greater interoperability with DSS would increase the efficiency with which the services interact with OSD regarding appointment and promotion scrolls. Error-detecting rules within existing programs, such as those used in AFRISS, could also increase efficiency and decrease errors.

Even with improvements to electronic systems, the services must address inefficiencies and error-generating steps within their processes. Most notably, the timelines associated with intercomponent transfers should be communicated to active duty officers long before they consider leaving active duty. Increased oversight within service personnel offices could also prevent last-minute scrolling requests when accession sources (such as ROTC units) neglect to submit scrolling paperwork in time before planned commissioning dates.

CHAPTER FOUR

Approaches to Reducing Rework

We visualize several broad approaches to reducing rework. After discussing these approaches in general, we outline specific steps that could be taken under either the current DSS or an enhanced DSS.

Broad Approaches

The three broad approaches we visualize are *increased accountability*, *increased automation*, and *streamlining appointment processes*.

Increased Accountability

Increased accountability would entail tracking the numbers and types of errors and providing the resulting error rates as feedback to upstream processors and higher-level officials. OEPM would track errors attributable to the scroll-providing elements within the services and components. Current methods include use of Word documents uploaded to the Access database, which is helpful but inefficient; updates to DSS should provide real-time feedback to the services. The scroll-providing elements at the service and component level would track errors attributable to commissioning sources, promotion management staffs, and other originators of appointment actions. Error rates would be provided periodically to appropriate authorities in service secretariat and headquarters staffs. Tracking error rates would provide an accountability mechanism by pinpointing poor performance and provide diagnostic benefits, such as quantifying the most common sources of error, guiding specific training needs, guiding process improvements, and identifying staffing inadequacies. Good error data would both motivate and guide investment in additional resources.

Increased Automation

OEPM personnel indicated that the current limitations of DSS have forced them to construct workarounds in the forms of auxiliary databases and email exchanges to provide the tracking and information flows that would be automated in an enhanced DSS.

The Air Force has demonstrated how increased automation can reduce both processing costs and errors. The Air Force's system for original appointments contains individual records for each appointee. Most entries are made through the use of drop-down menu lists, preventing format errors. The system also provides automatic checks for inconsistent relationships among various entries pertinent to an appointment. All coordination within the Air Force is accomplished electronically before the scroll is printed. All appointment scrolls are printed at a single point, just before delivery to OEPM.

All services have the potential to develop systems comparable with the Air Force system. However, a better solution would be to provide a DoD-wide system. Although OSD would bear the full expense, a single system likely would be less costly for DoD than multiple systems constructed by the military departments, military services, and multiple components within each service. This system would defer printing of a scroll until all coordination and quality assurance steps within OSD were completed.

Streamlining Appointment Processes

We see streamlining opportunities at both statutory and policy levels. At the statutory level, officer management processes would be streamlined by elimination of the distinction between regular and reserve appointments. This issue is treated at length in Chapter Five. At the policy level, the requirement to distinguish between civilians, enlisted members, and officers in the text of a scroll presents an unnecessary source of error. This information, if needed by OSD for processing the scroll, can be communicated electronically. Similarly, the specific grade of an officer being reappointed (the issue of appointment *in* versus *to* a grade) could be conveyed electronically rather than being embedded in the text of the scroll. In addition to eliminating sources of error on the printed scrolls, these policy changes would allow consolidation of what now must be separate scrolls for each of these variations.

Combining Multiple Avenues

The three avenues described here are not mutually exclusive. Elements of all three can be combined to improve appointment processes. A central consideration in merging multiple avenues is the degree to which the current DSS can be enhanced. Accordingly, we have developed two sets of potential improvements. One set can be implemented with the current DSS, and the other would need a version of DSS that could incorporate individual-level appointee records.

Process maps provided in Appendix B depict the expected general flow of packages within OSD with an improved DSS. Two other maps depict a generalized service-level flow using a standardized input workbook with the current DSS and service-level flows with an enhanced DSS.

Enhancements with Current DSS

The current DSS is not designed to include individual-level records or to transfer individual-level data between scroll-processing activities. Accordingly, DSS as currently configured plays a very limited role in reducing errors in individual-level information contained on scrolls. Systematic error reduction must be done outside DSS.

Two potential enhancements are not dependent on DSS. The first is a shift to the DoD identification number (also known as the Electronic Data Interchange Person Identifier), instead of the name or SSN, as the key identifier of an individual to be placed on a scroll. The second is the use of a standardized Excel file as an input for scroll production and as a searchable companion and individual-level data repository accompanying each scroll. A process map provided in Appendix B illustrates how processes could flow within the military departments with a scroll input file incorporated as part of the process.

Defense Enrollment Eligibility Reporting System and the Department of Defense Identification Number

Using the DoD identification number as the primary identifier for individuals on a scroll provides multiple benefits. First, it eliminates use of the truncated SSN, which is inadequate on its own to uniquely identify an individual. This step would bring scroll production into conformity with DoDI 1000.30, which prescribes reduced use of the SSN. Second, it allows the Defense Enrollment Eligibility Reporting System (DEERS) to serve its intended purpose as the authoritative data source for identify and verification of affiliation with DoD. Third, because DEERS is the authoritative source for names of DoD-affiliated personnel, electronically transcribing names from DEERS to scrolls would virtually eliminate name errors on original appointment scrolls. Fourth, DEERS would provide all current and past military affiliations of an individual, eliminating some grade and military status errors in original appointment scrolls and related documentation.

Our enhanced process envisions an automated process for service personnel to retrieve DEERS data. Service personnel constructing appointment scroll packages would feed a list of DoD identification numbers of appointment candidates to DEERS and receive a formatted report providing names in appropriate format for a scroll, prior military affiliations, and other information on each candidate. The report either would be formatted to form the basis of a proposed scroll preparation worksheet or would provide a source that could be easily transcribed electronically to a scroll preparation worksheet. DEERS points of contact have indicated that this process could be automated at the DEERS end.

Most individuals appearing on original appointment scrolls would be registered in DEERS before the point at which a scroll package is assembled. Service academy students, ROTC scholarship recipients, and individuals attending Officer Training School or OCS fall into this category. Others would have to visit a Real-Time Automated Personnel Identification System (RAPIDS) site (e.g., any military or dependent identification card-issuing activity) or their commissioning sources would have to establish a RAPIDS site. RAPIDS sites are manned by operators trained to capture identification data from valid sources. This would eliminate the need for further verification of identity information by scroll package assemblers, who might not be appropriately trained for this task. In addition, DEERS provides a mechanism for individual appointees to review and correct their names or any other identity information before a scroll is prepared.

Scroll List Worksheet

Processing efficiency and error-catching could be enhanced by requiring a standard Excel worksheet. This worksheet would contain a row for each individual that will be included on a scroll, along with fields for the information to appear on the scroll (as well as fields for other supporting information). The worksheet could be modeled after the product currently used by the Air Force, which contains data validation edits for the fields contained in the worksheet (see Appendix C). As described earlier, policy could prescribe that names, DoD identifications, SSNs, and other fields be transcribed or derived electronically from a DEERS output report instead of being rekeyed into this worksheet.

The worksheet would be used by reviewers at every stage of the process and would be uploaded to the OEPM DSS, along with other scroll package documents. It would allow electronic inspection of the scroll data in place of visual inspection of material in the printed scroll. In addition, names that were dropped from a scroll could be retained in the worksheet, with remarks and coded fields used to document the reason for the deletion. Overall, the worksheet would provide an improved history of actions affecting a scroll.

To maximize scroll inspection efficiency and electronic transfer of scroll package materials, the scroll would be printed at the latest possible stage of the process. The worksheet would be used as an input for a merge procedure to produce the printed scroll.[1] For actions requiring Senate confirmation, the same procedure could be used to produce the

---

1 In the case of the Air Force, the worksheet provided for this purpose would not be the same one used as an AFRISS input; doing so would bypass the error-catching relationship edits embedded in AFRISS. Instead, it would be an AFRISS output after all reviews and coordinations were completed.

Senate text file. Ideally, production would occur within OSD, either in OEPM or Washington Headquarters Services. This shift in workload, besides being more efficient, would burden the OSD staff rather than the services to prepare material for exercise of authority by the Secretary or Deputy Secretary of Defense.

If standard preparation worksheets and merge documents are adopted but printed production remains a responsibility of the services, we would recommend including the preparation worksheet in scroll packages as an accountability enhancement. The scroll package record in DSS could retain the name of the individual who printed the scroll and the specific version of the preparation worksheet that was used.

Process maps (as provided in Appendix B) show use of the scroll preparation worksheet for original appointment processes. For original appointment scrolls, regardless of where they are printed (by OSD or by the services), we believe use of standardized preparation worksheets would substantially reduce rework. The advantage of using the worksheet would be very limited for promotion processes if scrolls are printed by the services because the data supporting the scroll generally are already in service personnel databases. However, if the process changes to allow printing of promotion scrolls at OSD, the worksheet would provide a vehicle to convey the scroll data from the services to OSD.

Service-Level Data Systems

In addition to adoption of a standardized scroll list worksheet, the services could be encouraged to adopt an online scroll preparation system similar to the one embedded by the Air Force in AFRISS. One advantage of an online system is the potential to apply relationship edits between fields in the scroll list worksheet. These relationship edits enforce compatibility between certain fields (e.g., "if current rank or current military status are populated, both must be populated"). (The relationship edits used in the Air Force system are shown in Appendix D.) Another advantage is that scroll lists could be coordinated within a service headquarters, with printing occurring only after all coordination and any resulting changes in the scroll list have been completed.

If OSD were to adopt an improved DSS with entity-level representation of individuals, service-level systems might be unnecessary. With an appropriate design, an OSD system could provide data validation and relationship edits, allow coordination within service headquarters as well as OSD, and allow printing after all coordination is complete.

Eliminating Noncritical Scroll Distinctions

In addition to names, truncated SSNs, and appointment grade, the following three required scroll distinctions are common sources of error:

1. distinction between individual (i.e., no current military service affiliation), enlisted member, and officer
2. distinction between appointment *in* or *to* the grade
3. section numbers in Title 10 that are cited as authority for the appointments.

The first two distinctions could be eliminated from the header text appearing on scrolls, avoiding errors that currently require reprinting of scrolls and allowing fewer separate scrolls. In a scroll's header text, the term *individual* could serve inclusively for all three of the currently differentiated person types. Appointment *in* a grade also could be understood to pertain to both those who currently hold the specified grade and those who are newly appointed to serve in that grade. Notably, use of *in* for all appointments would make scroll wording consistent with statutory appointment language, wherein all references to officer appointments related to promotions uniformly use *in* rather than *to* the grade (see 10 U.S.C. §624 and §12203). If these distinctions are needed for administrative or scroll processing purposes, they can be carried in the scroll preparation worksheet, where they can be easily corrected without scroll rework.

The third distinction—Title 10 section numbers—might be better placed in a memo, scroll preparation worksheet, or other documentation accompanying a scroll rather than on the scroll itself. Any errors in citing the appointment authority are more easily corrected in the accompanying material than on the scroll itself.

With these distinctions eliminated, the header text could uniformly read as follows for Secretarial signature:

> In accordance with the authorities extended to me under Title 10, United States Code, I hereby appoint the following individual(s) in the grade(s) indicated in the {military service}:

The header text could uniformly read as follows for Presidential signature:

> In accordance with Title 10, United States Code, I nominate the following individual(s) for appointment in the grade(s) indicated in the {military service}:

Eliminating Reappointment for Within-Service Occupational Changes

Another distinction, which is not in itself a source of error but which creates additional work, is found in the Army and Navy portions of Title 10 requiring appointments that are specific to Army basic or special branches (10 U.S.C. §7064 and §7153) and Navy line or staff corps (10 U.S.C. §8132). Movement between these branches or corps requires reappointment. Although the Air Force and the Marine Corps have similar occupational distinctions, reappointment is not required. Rather, officers are reassigned among comparable occupational groups under the general authority of and pursuant to regulations prescribed by service secretaries.

Source Documentation

The services should maintain a database for storing electronic copies of individuals' Social Security cards as the authoritative source for names and identities. The services should then require the originator of an appointment scroll package to verify each name on the scroll against the Social Security card. At the service level, the scrolling office should then spot-check the scrolls sent from the personnel centers.

Enhanced Error Tracking

Although streamlining can eliminate many errors that force reworking of scrolls, it is unlikely to eliminate all errors. To further improve scrolling processes, we recommend maintaining a more structured and more detailed categorization and history of scroll errors to provide a basis for enhanced performance feedback to the services.

Our recommended framework would include a four-part field recorded at the package level.

The first part would indicate the severity of the error. Two code values might be sufficient for this field: *corrected by OSD* or *returned to service for correction*. The second part would indicate the nature of the error. This might include errors such as *U.S.C. section number* (if retained as part of the scroll or the package), *incorrect appointment grade,* and *missing prior appointment.* An *other* error code could be included for use with narrative comments, but all common error conditions should be codified. Doing so simplifies data entry and readily enables compilation of data on various error types. A third part could indicate the office that detected the error, with such code values as *OEPM*, *OGC*, *Office of the Secretary*, and *other.* The package-level error fields should allow multiple entries because multiple error types might be found in the same package. The fourth part would automatically add an entry date for tracking purposes.

Additionally, with a scroll preparation worksheet, fields could be provided to flag individuals for whom an error is identified or suspected. Like the package-level error codes, the individual-level error flags, with additional comments if needed, would identify the nature of the error. An additional field can be provided to signal that action has been taken either by OSD or by the responsible service to address the error. Again, to accommodate multiple errors on an individual record, multiple-occurrence fields might be needed for each record.

Coded fields in DSS, ancillary databases, and scroll preparation worksheets could reduce rework. They would also streamline OSD's review and processing of scroll packages. Current processes require narrative entries, email correspondence, or phone calls to convey error information to the services. With coded data field entries, error information could be quickly recorded and transmitted to the services.

Enhancements with an Improved DSS

With improvements in DSS, data on individuals to be included on a scroll would be recorded in individual-level records contained in DSS itself. To permit efficient movement of names and other data from service-level systems, DSS should be configured to accept either individual manual updates to individual records or an electronic input file, similar to the scroll list worksheet described earlier. The latter would be particularly useful, for example, to transfer lists from service personnel data or promotion management systems. Process maps provided in Appendix B illustrate how processes could flow within OSD and the military departments with an enhanced DSS. An enhanced DSS would eliminate the need for ancillary databases for tracking errors in package-level information not carried in the current DSS, including the package-level error codes mentioned above. It also would allow individual-level error codes to be recorded within DSS rather than on the scroll list worksheet recommended for use in the current system. This would allow the services to continually monitor and react to errors rather than rely on an electronic worksheet from OEPM.

CHAPTER FIVE

Eliminating Reappointment of Officers Transferring Between Components

Under current statutes, appointment of officers is specific to the active or reserve membership of an armed force. This specificity derives from the different statutory authorities in Title 10 regarding appointment of regular and reserve officers. Provisions pertaining to regular officers are predominantly in Subtitle A (General Military Law); those pertaining to reserve officers are predominantly in Subtitle D (Reserve Components).[1] As indicated in previous chapters, services report that transfers between components account for 25 percent to 33 percent of original appointment scrolls. Cross-component appointments present large workloads in themselves and are prone to errors that require rework, particularly in cases where an officer is simultaneously awaiting a component transfer and a promotion.

In its report on the FY 2020 NDAA, the U.S. Senate Committee on Armed Services (SASC) noted that

> each of the military departments has expressed a desire to expedite the transfer of officers between the active and reserve components. One hurdle in the current transfer process is the requirement for separate appointments into each component (SASC, 2019, p. 156).

The FY 2020 NDAA required a report from the Secretary of Defense regarding the frequency with which this hurdle is encountered and an assessment of options for removing it.

---

1 Specific references to regular and reserve appointments in Title 10 are addressed in Appendix E.

To avoid the need for separate appointments, Title 10 can be changed in either of two ways envisaged in the FY 2020 NDAA reporting requirement. The first—what might be called a *dual-appointment* approach—would leave most of the appointment provisions of Title 10 unchanged but would add a provision that deems an appointment of one type to also be an appointment of the opposite type. A second approach—a *consolidating* approach—would eliminate distinctions between regular and reserve appointments. This would require excising references to regular-specific or reserve-specific appointments or grades throughout Title 10 and revising various provisions as necessary to establish a single type of appointment applicable to service as either an active or a reserve officer. In the remainder of this chapter, we describe the limitations of a dual-appointment approach, then provide the definitional foundations and proposed changes needed for a consolidating approach.

In its original version of the FY 2020 NDAA, the SASC put forth a dual-appointment approach (see 10 U.S.C. §502). The provision would have amended §12203 of Title 10, which pertains to reserve appointments, to include the following:

> For purposes of appointments under this section, an officer who receives an original appointment as a regular commissioned officer in a grade under section 531 of this title that is made on or after the date of the enactment of the National Defense Authorization Act for Fiscal Year 2020 shall be deemed also to have received an original appointment as a reserve commissioned officer in such grade.

After consideration by the House and Senate conferences, this provision was dropped. In its place, the final legislation carried the reporting requirement (§501) described above.

The dual-appointment approach would present the following problems:

- Appointments are made in or to a specific grade. In addition to deeming an original active appointment to also be a reserve appointment, all active promotion appointments would have to be deemed to be reserve promotion appointments. Otherwise, officers transferring from regular to reserve service would require an appointment in the appropriate grade at the time of the transfer, eliminating the gain in administrative efficiency made by dual original appointments.

- Because Title 10 would continue to distinguish between regular and reserve grades, a regular officer originally appointed in a regular grade would presumably also hold the corresponding reserve grade. However, without a provision for dual appointment to promotion grades, regular officers who are promoted in their regular grade would continue to hold the reserve grade in which they were originally appointed.
- Clarifications would be required to establish that although regular officers would hold a reserve appointment and a reserve grade, they would not be members of a reserve component, would not be considered a reserve officer or a *Reserve* (as defined in §101 and §10141—see discussion in the "Duty Status" section), and would not actually appear on or compete for promotion on the reserve active-status list. Without these clarifications, these officers might be subject to both regular and reserve active duty and active status strength and grade constraints.
- In the particular approach advanced by the SASC, the need for reappointment would be eliminated for one direction of transfer—from active to reserve—but not for transfers in the opposite direction. If officers with dual appointments were allowed to retain their regular appointments after transferring to a reserve component, a partial reserve-to-active permeability enhancement would be realized. However, it is unclear that retaining a regular appointment (including continued appointment in a corresponding regular grade after promotion in a reserve grade) would be acceptable under those circumstances. Also, the approach would not provide any improvement in reappointment ease for officers originally appointed in a reserve component.
- Personnel data systems would need to be expanded to track which reserve officers have only a reserve appointment and which have both regular and reserve appointments. Expansion of personnel

databases would be required so that active and reserve grades and dates of rank could be recorded and tracked for each officer.
- The SASC proposal would affect only future appointments, leaving the administrative burdens of officer transfers between components in place for many years to come.

A consolidating approach involves more-sweeping changes, but it allows important component-specific provisions relating to appointment, promotion, and separation processes to remain unambiguous. In particular, the changed provisions could continue to support distinctions between *active duty* and *active status*, between the *active duty list* and the *reserve active status list*, between membership in a *regular component* and a *reserve component*, and between a *regular officer* and a *reserve officer*. These distinctions are used throughout Title 10 to specify which officers are subject to the provisions of a particular section. None of these four distinctions has exactly the same statutory meaning, but a dual-appointment approach to facilitating transfers could leave them muddied, threatening the clarity of statutory requirements for officer management.

Definitions

To provide a foundation for a proposed consolidating approach, we review definitions of certain terms and, where needed, propose changes to the definitions.

Components

Components are clearly specified in Title 10. Table 5.1 provides the complete list of DoD components.

Duty Status

Active duty is defined in §101 as full-time duty in active military service. All regular military members are on active duty. Reservists could be on active duty in two ways: either as reservists called to active duty under various provisions of Title 10 or as *active Guard and Reserve*

Table 5.1
Components of the Military Departments

Department	Active Components	Reserve Components
Army	• Regular Army	• Army National Guard of the United States • Army Reserve
Navy	• Regular Navy • Regular Marine Corps	• Navy Reserve • Marine Corps Reserve
Air Force	• Regular Air Force • Regular Space Force[a]	• Air National Guard of the United States • Air Force Reserve

SOURCES: 10 U.S.C. §101, §7062, §8001, §9062, and §10101.
[a] The Space Force was created as a provision of the FY 2020 NDAA. At the time of writing, reserve components of the Space Force had not been designated.

members serving under the provisions of §12301(d) and §12310 of Title 10 or §502(f) of Title 32.

Reservists could also be in *active, inactive,* or *retired* status. §101 defines active status to be that of a member of a reserve component who is not in an inactive status. According to §10141, active and inactive status for reservists is tied to their placement in a Ready Reserve, a Standby Reserve, or a Retired Reserve. Inactive status is that of designated reservists in the Standby Reserve, in the inactive Army National Guard, or in the inactive Air Force National Guard. Reservists in the Retired Reserve are in a retired status. All other reservists, including those on active duty, are in an active status.

Regular Versus Reserve

The terms *regular* and *reserve* are defined in §101 in interlocking ways. The term *reserve* (common noun) pertains to "enlistment, appointment, grade, or office held as a Reserve [proper noun] of one of the armed forces." The term *Reserve,* in turn, is defined indirectly in §10141 as a member of a Ready Reserve, a Standby Reserve, or a Retired Reserve. The term *regular* pertains to "enlistment, appointment, grade, or office in a regular component of an armed force." However, since reservists could remain reservists while serving in various regular-component capacities, the definition of the term *regular* could be read to include them. An unambiguous definition of *regular* would use a partial negative, defining it as pertaining to a member serving on active duty who is *not a Reserve.*

A consolidated change to Title 10 would include removing the distinctions between regular and reserve appointments and grades. Accordingly, our recommended changes remove the terms *appointment* and *grade* from these definitions. They also incorporate the explicitly defined term *Reserve* in the definition of *regular.*

Active Duty List Versus Reserve Active-Status List

The *active duty list* and the *reserve active-status list* are defined and maintained for the purpose of considering officers for promotion in the separate systems established for regular and reserve officers. However, the two lists do not divide cleanly along a boundary between regular and reserve. The active duty list is defined in §101 as "a single list . . . which contains the names of all officers of [an] armed force, other than officers described in section 641 of this title, who are serving on active duty." §641 lists various categories of officers, including reservists called to or serving on active duty who are not subject to active-duty strength and grade limitations or the normal promotion and separation provisions pertaining to active-duty officers.[2] The reserve active-status list is "a single list . . . that contains the names of all officers of [an] armed force . . . who are in an active status in a reserve component . . . and are not on an active-duty list."

2 These exceptions cover most but not out all reserve officers serving on active duty. For example, §641(1)(A) makes an exception for officers who are "excluded from counting for active-duty end strengths under §115(i) of this title." However, §115(b)(2) specifies that reservists called to active duty for a period of greater than three years or on active duty for more than 1,095 days in the preceding 1,460 days are counted in active-duty strengths. They are thus transferred to the active-duty list unless an exception is made by the service secretary under §620(d). Exceptions to the active-duty list also cover some small categories of regular officers, such as directors of admissions, deans, and permanent professors at military academies.

Proposed Changes for a Consolidating Approach

Appendix E provides line-in/line-out changes that would be needed for a consolidating approach. The general approach is to make the original appointment provisions in Subtitle A applicable to both active and reserve officers and to remove most original appointment provisions from Subtitle D. With these changes, there would cease to be a distinction between a regular commission and a reserve commission. Accordingly, the *regular* and *reserve* modifiers would be removed from any reference to a commission, appointment, or grade.

Although a consolidating approach would eliminate a distinction between active and reserve grades, retaining a separate promotion system for reservists (including retention on a reserve active-status list while serving on active duty) serves an important purpose. A separate system would allow reservists to continue to compete against their reserve-component peers who are not on active duty. It would also prevent hampering active-duty promotion boards by forcing board members to compare the records of reserve members serving on active duty with their regular counterparts, given the dissimilarities between regular and reserve career paths. Because reservists would likely suffer in such comparisons, a separate promotion board would keep tours on active duty attractive to reservists.

The active-duty list, the reserve active-status list, and the promotion procedures associated with them provide different paths toward appointment in a higher grade, but the appointments do not have to be differentiated as active or reserve appointments. In the current framework, multiple statutory authorities lead to either a regular or a reserve appointment in a particular grade. For example, regular officers can be appointed to a higher grade under §531 as an original appointment with constructive credit, §624 as a normal promotion, or under the various sections pertaining to military academy permanent professions and directors of admissions. Similarly, in a consolidated framework, regular and reserve promotion provisions would both provide several different authorities, each supporting undifferentiated appointment to a higher grade.

Consolidating appointments does not imply that all officers would automatically be accepted for transfer from one component to another. It does imply that they would transfer in the same grade, subject to the seniority adjustments specified in §741(d)(3). We have included a proposed §12216 to clarify that transfers would be subject to regulations and requirements and that, with some exceptions, officers would retain grade and seniority when transferred between components (although our changes are not strictly required for a consolidating approach).

Transitional Provisions

Consolidation of statutory distinctions between regular and reserve appointments, grades, and commissions requires some transitional language. Our recommended changes in Appendix E contain such provisions for §531, §624, and §12203. However, because §12203 does not refer specifically to *reserve* grade or *reserve* appointments, transitional language might be unnecessary for that section.

Inconsistencies Regarding Senate Confirmation

For appointments related to promotions, §624 requires Senate confirmation for appointment of regular officers in the grade of O-4 and above; §12203 requires Senate confirmation for appointment of reserve officers in the grade of O-6 and above. With consolidation of appointments, this inconsistency could result in reservists in grades O-4 and O-5 transferring to the active duty list or to service as regular officers and serving in that capacity without Senate confirmation.

We see the following four possibilities for resolving this inconsistency:

- Revise §624 to require Senate confirmation for appointment of regular officers only at grades O-6 and above.
- Revise §12203 to require Senate confirmation for appointment of reserve officers at grades O-4 and above.
- Let the inconsistent provisions stand. The requirement for Senate confirmation of appointment at various grades would be based on whether the officer is a Reserve at the time of the appointment. With or without Senate confirmation, the appointment in a com-

missioned grade would be valid for service as a regular or reserve officer in either a regular or a reserve component.

- Let the inconsistent provisions stand, but require Senate confirmation of a previous promotion appointment at the time a reserve O-4 or O-5 is considered for a transfer to active duty. Under this option, the Senate would be confirming an appointment that was previously tendered and accepted.

Of these four options, the first seems preferable. It would reduce administrative burdens on all parties involved in Senate confirmations. It would also remove the implication that regular officers require more congressional scrutiny than reserve officers to serve in the grades of O-4 and O-5. Although we have not incorporated either the first or the second option in our proposed changes in Appendix E, the changes needed to implement the first option would be straightforward. The second option might require transitional provisions to account for reservists appointed to grades O-4 and O-5 without Senate confirmation prior to the change. The fourth option seems especially problematic in that it could lead to retroactive invalidation of a previously tendered appointment.

Warrant Officers

Title 10 places matters pertaining to the appointment, promotion, and separation of warrant officers completely under the authority of the secretary concerned. In addition, Chapter 1207, pertaining to reserve warrant officers, contains only minimal material requiring change to make regular warrant officer provisions applicable in the reserve components. Therefore, consolidation of appointment provisions is not needed to reduce administrative burdens. However, if consolidation to remove distinctions between regular and reserve commissioned officer appointments and grades is adopted, comparable changes might be useful to eliminate distinctions between regular and reserve warrant officer appointments and grades.

Enlistments

Title 10 does not distinguish between regular and reserve enlistments. Chapter 31, found in the General Military Law subtitle, pertains generally to all enlistments with only certain sections designated as applicable to enlistment in regular components. Chapter 1201, under the Reserve Components subtitle, contains the necessary provisions to account for issues unique to reserve service. Accordingly, no consolidating changes are needed in these chapters.

Recommendations

If a consolidating approach is not favored, we would recommend a dual-appointment approach similar to the one proposed by the SASC. However, we would expand the scope of the dual-appointment language to include both original and promotion appointments and to make the equivalent regular and reserve appointments retroactive rather than prospective. Without this expansion of scope, the military departments and OSD would continue to bear a heavy administrative burden well into the future (in the case of original appointments) or indefinitely (in the case of promotion appointments).

However, as we demonstrate through the changes outlined in Appendix E, a consolidating approach is manageable. It creates the greatest clarity for implementation by OSD and the services. It also reduces the likelihood of unintended consequences as a result of applying conflicting statutory requirements in unforeseen ways and to unforeseen circumstances.

CHAPTER SIX

Conclusions and Recommendations

We have observed frustrations with the scrolling process within both the military departments and OEPM. OEPM notes high error rates for packages and attributes them to insufficient quality assurance processes within the military departments. The military departments find the nuanced requirements of the scrolling process difficult to meet with consistency because of the number of variables that differentiate appointment packages and a general lack of automated processes that would help find or avoid errors.

Conclusions

Rework increases workloads and delays processing at all levels. In addition, the resulting processing delays can adversely affect appointees. Some rework could be avoided through greater diligence on the part of the service and departmental staffs processing scrolling packages. We also note that some error-inducing administrative requirements are unnecessary and that current automated systems are less than ideal for reducing errors and increasing efficiency.

Transitioning from an active to a reserve component is especially troublesome. Individual officers separating from active duty might not be aware of the need for a reserve appointment or of the lead time required to obtain it. Pending promotions further complicate the process, possibly requiring multiple scrolls to complete the transition in the appropriate grade. The resulting breaks in service could adversely affect appointees' interests.

Graduation from medical education programs provides another troublesome point. Depending on the program, an officer might be changing both components and grades simultaneously or almost simultaneously. Scrolling errors can adversely affect these graduates' compensation and relocation benefits.

Recommendations

We recommend the following three broad approaches to reducing rework:

1. **increased accountability**: providing more-complete feedback to the military departments on the types and frequency of errors
2. **increased automation**: using data processing to implement error-avoiding and error-trapping rules
3. **streamlining appointment processes**: eliminating rescrolling requirements when moving between regular and reserve components or between branches or corps within a service, and eliminating unnecessary distinctions in scroll headers, such as those that require separate scrolls for officers, enlisted members, and civilians.

These approaches could be implemented to some extent using the current DSS, but they would be much more readily accommodated in an improved DSS.

With the current DSS, the following specific enhancements would be possible:

- using the DoD identification number in place of the SSN as the unique person identifier; in addition to using DoD's preferred person identifier, this would allow use of the DEERS as an authoritative source of names, including suffixes and middle initials, and prior military affiliations

- using an Excel-based scroll worksheet, with field validation rules, as a source to print scrolls at the latest possible point in the scroll production process
- at OEPM and within the services, at the service level, adopting online scroll preparation systems similar to the one used by the Air Force
- implementing the streamlining changes described above
- capturing images of Social Security account cards as part of the source documentation for appointment packages at the service level (if SSNs continue to be used as person identifiers)
- at OEPM and within the services, maintaining sufficient error data to permit identification and diagnosis of prevailing problems.

With an improved DSS, these enhancements could be much more easily and comprehensively implemented. Coordination within the services and OSD could be done through searchable, easily circulated electronic files. Printing of scrolls could be deferred until all review, coordination, and corrective actions have been completed.

References

Department of Defense Directive 1344.10, "Political Activities by Members of the Armed Forces," Washington, D.C., February 9, 2008.

Department of Defense Instruction 1310.02, *Original Appointment of Officers*, Washington, D.C., March 26, 2015.

Department of Defense Instruction 1320.04, *Military Officer Actions Requiring Presidential, Secretary of Defense, or Under Secretary of Defense for Personnel Readiness Approval or Senate Confirmation*, Washington, D.C., January 3, 2014.

DoDI—*See* U.S. Department of Defense Instruction.

GAO—*See* Government Accountability Office.

Government Accountability Office, *Military Personnel: Factors Affecting Approval Time for Officer Appointments,* Washington, D.C., GAO-19-527R, April 3, 2019. As of August 31, 2020:
https://www.gao.gov/assets/710/700056.pdf

Marine Administrative Message 080/11, "Process for Officers Transitioning from the Active Duty List (ADL) to the Reserve Active Status List (RASL) and Individuals Requesting to Be Reappointed to the RASL," Arlington, Va., February 3, 2011. As of September 30, 2020:
https://www.marines.mil/News/Messages/Messages-Display/Article/888377/process-for-officers-transitioning-from-the-active-duty-list-adl-to-the-reserve

Marine Corps Recruiting Command Order 1100.2A, *Marine Corps Recruiting Command Officer Commissioning Manual*, Quantico, Va., January 11, 2016. As of August 31, 2020:
https://www.mcrc.marines.mil/Portals/95/MCRCO%201100.2A%20(OCM).PDF

National Guard Association of the United States, "Government Report Examines FEDREC Process," webpage, July 2, 2019. As of March 31, 2020:
https://www.ngaus.org/about-ngaus/newsroom/government-report-examines-fedrec-process

Navy Personnel Command Career Transition Office, "Officer Active Component to Reserve Component (AC2RC) Transition," webpage, undated. As of October 23, 2020:
https://www.public.navy.mil/bupers-npc/career/transition/Pages/Officer.aspx

Navy Personnel Command Instruction 5400.1A, *Navy Personnel Command Organization Manual,* Millington, Tenn., 2015. As of April 14, 2020:
https://www.mynavyhr.navy.mil/Portals/55/Reference/Instructions/NPC/NPCI_5400.1.pdf

Navy Personnel Command Manual 1131-040, *Appointment of Officers in the Navy Reserve*, Millington, Tenn., 2013. As of October 23, 2020:
https://www.mynavyhr.navy.mil/Portals/55/Reference/MILPERSMAN/1000/1100Recruiting/1131-040.pdf?ver=IMnhoHGqjONXD0xSd1zfvA%3d%3d

SASC—*See* U.S. Senate Committee on Armed Services.

U.S. Code, Title 10, Armed Forces. As of September 9, 2020:
https://www.govinfo.gov/content/pkg/CPRT-112HPRT67342/pdf/CPRT-112HPRT67342.pdf

U.S. Department of Defense, "Changes Roll Out for Transition Assistance Program," press release, September 30, 2019. As of May 12, 2020:
https://www.defense.gov/Explore/News/Article/Article/1975250/changes-roll-out-for-transition-assistance-program

U.S. Senate Committee on Armed Services, *National Defense Authorization Act for Fiscal Year 2020*, Washington, D.C., June 11, 2019. As of March 13, 2021:
https://www.congress.gov/116/crpt/srpt48/CRPT-116srpt48.pdf